DAVID KNOWLES

PROFESSOR THE REV. M. D. KNOWLES

Michael Noakes
1961

DOM ADRIAN MOREY

DAVID KNOWLES

A Memoir

Darton, Longman & Todd
London

First published in Great Britain in 1979 by
Darton, Longman & Todd Ltd
89 Lillie Road
London SW6 1UD

© 1979 Adrian Morey

ISBN 0 232 51435 6

Printed in Great Britain by The Anchor Press Ltd
and bound by Wm. Brendon & Son Ltd,
both of Tiptree, Essex

CONTENTS

PREFACE

The appointment of a Regius Professor of Modern History is made by the Prime Minister of the day, and his choice, in modern times at least, is made normally from scholars who have passed their working life in academic surroundings. Two holders of the Cambridge Chair have been exceptional. The first, Lord Acton, had never been a member of an English university and in his inaugural lecture recalled that, as a Roman Catholic, three Cambridge colleges had refused him admission. David Knowles was appointed by Winston Churchill and was the first Benedictine monk to hold the Chair. The unusual circumstances that brought him to a life outside the cloister stimulated an interest and a curiosity which still exist, and now that those associated with the controversial period of his life are dead the story can be told.

This memoir is drawn mainly from material in the archives of Downside Abbey and was not originally intended for publication, hence there are a number of personal references that would otherwise have been omitted. I have been urged to let them stand, and indeed they show how two friends, both with much the same interests and ideals, could interpret the same facts and possibilities connected with their calling in differing ways.

My thanks are due in the first place to the Abbot of Downside who allowed me to use the Abbey archives without which the story could not have been told, to Professor C. N. L. Brooke and Dom Alberic Stacpoole for permission to use their articles published in the *Proceedings of the British Academy* and in the *Ampleforth Journal*. I have also been aided by the Abbot of Quarr, Professor Sir Herbert Butterfield, and Brian Wormald, Fellow of Peterhouse. David Knowles left an autobiography but his literary executor decided that it was not to be published or opened to inspection for some years to come. I have therefore been unable to quote from it. I have, however, had the benefit of the recollections of Dame Katharine Loxton, a childhood companion, and of Dom Mark Pontifex, Librarian of Downside Abbey and an exact contemporary both in the school and in the community. Lastly, my thanks are due to the Syndics of the Cambridge University Press for permission to quote from the writings of David Knowles, to Lord Clark, who has allowed me to quote from *The Other Half*, and to the Master and Fellows of Peterhouse for permission to reproduce the Noakes drawing as frontispiece.

Adrian Morey
November 1978

Chapter One

HISTORICAL BACKGROUND

The English Congregation has been largely determined
in its work by its early history.
                                        D. K., *Christian Monasticism*, 1969

Twelve miles beyond Bath to the South West lie Downside
Abbey and School; a traveller along the Fosse Way will
see the tower of the Abbey church rising ahead on a crest
of the Mendip hills. David Knowles spent nearly thirty
years of his life at Downside, first as a boy in its school and
then as a member of its monastic community. Those who
knew him well during his academic life at Cambridge were
well aware of the deep impression those years had made
on his life and outlook and of the extent to which they
coloured his work as a historian. For him Downside
always remained a place of predilection. Therefore no
apology is needed for a brief outline of the story of what in
many ways was a remarkable religious community.

In the final volume of his work, *The Religious Orders of
England, The Tudor Age,* its author did not end his story
with the dissolution of the monasteries but with a section
entitled 'Reaction and Survival'. This not only covered the
Marian restoration of Westminster Abbey but also, and
this was something new, dealt with the revival of English
monasticism that came about in the last years of
Elizabeth's reign. An element almost of romance was provided by the shadowy figure of Dom Sigebert Buckley, the

1

David Knowles

last surviving member of Marian Westminster, who had witnessed to his faith during long years of imprisonment ending with the accession of James I. His existence was used by Englishmen at Rome to persuade Clement VIII that English monks in foreign monasteries should be allowed to return as missionaries to their native land. Here in Buckley was 'the living testimony to the continuity of their faith and to the antiquity of the Roman obedience'. It took some twenty years to secure the permission, but in the winter of 1603–4 two English monks of the Italian Cassinese Congregation landed in England and later, with some formal ceremonial, were aggregated by Buckley to the Westminster community. It was believed that, as the last surviving member of a corporate body, he could thus pass on the canonical rights and privileges of pre-Reformation English monasticism. Advice on the legal aspect was given by Augustine Baker, a lawyer of distinction.

Shortly before these two English monks landed three others had arrived from Spain. They came from abbeys of the Spanish Congregation of Valladolid and were members of a fairly large group of English monks who were soon able to form their own community at Douai. The first novice was received there in 1607. At this time Philip de Caverel, Abbot of the great monastery at Arras, was building a college in Douai for his student monks who were studying at the University. He took the little English community under his wing and built on to his own college accommodation for them and a school for English boys. Thus the present Downside community had its beginning and in 1619 its generous benefactor gave a permanent endowment. In that year this community of St Gregory joined with other foundations to form a revived English Benedictine Congregation.

The Douai community of St Gregory was fortunate in the influences which combined to mould its tradition. First came that of the Spanish Congregation of Valladolid, a reformed group of monasteries with a very high standard

of studies. Its English members had shared a strict formation and the ablest of them had been sent to study at the
University of Salamanca. Second came the influence of the
Abbey of Arras, a community praised for its observance
by the two Maurists, Dom Martène and Dom Durand,
who visited there in 1718. (Second *Voyage litéraire de deux
Bénédictins,* 1724, pp. 62–72.) At Douai the English monks
lived apart from the Arras wing of the buildings but
taught the Abbey's young monks. They were fortunate in
this close association with an influential and observant
monastery.

From its earliest days this community of St Gregory
numbered men of distinction, and a surprising number of
its members have found their way into the *Dictionary of
National Biography.* There were the two 'founders', Augustine Bradshaw and John Roberts, both former monks of
the Abbey of St Martin at Compostella; the first died as
the reformer of a French Cluniac monastery and the second on the scaffold at Tyburn. Augustine Bradshaw established two other communities at Dieulouard in Lorraine
and at St Malo, was involved with the Spanish ambas-
sador in the scheme to buy toleration for the English
Catholics, and had talks with Sir Robert Cecil. Two men
governed the monastery in turn from 1612 to 1633: Leander Jones and Rudesind Barlow, both of whom were doc-
tors of Salamanca and held professorial chairs in the University of Douai. Leander Jones had been a friend and
contemporary of Laud at St John's College, Oxford, and
corresponded with the leading English antiquarians.
Rudesind Barlow published a book on papal authority
which was formally condemned by Rome. Another interesting personality, though not a member of the community, was Augustine Baker, who was on friendly terms with
Sir Robert Cotton, Spellman, Camden and Archbishop
Usher. From 1634 to 1638 he lived with the Douai community and acted as spiritual guide to many of its members, sometimes to the discomfort of the Prior. It was a
Gregorian, Dom Serenus Cressy, a former chaplain of

Lord Strafford, who edited Baker's spiritual writings, published in 1635 under the title of *Sancta Sophia*, or *Holy Wisdom*. Cressy also edited several works of the English medieval mystical writers, an interest shared throughout his life by David Knowles who in his turn was greatly influenced by the writings of Augustine Baker.

From the beginning the standard of ecclesiastical studies was a high one. Leander Jones was an orientalist and Professor of Hebrew in the University of Douai. He was the editor-in-chief of the *Biblia Sacra cum Glossa*, in six folio volumes, and supplied its Hebrew and Greek textual notes. He also shared with Augustine Baker in the collection of material for the *Apostolatus Benedictinorum in Anglia*, edited by Dom Clement Reyner and published in 1626. Apart from learned studies the community was occupied from its earliest days in two important activities. The greater number of the monks spent periods of missionary activity in England and by the end of the seventeenth century several had died on the scaffold or suffered imprisonment for their priesthood. By 1618 a school had been opened for the sons of English Catholics. In general, these seventeenth-century monks appear as radical, independent and opposed to political Catholicism; some were anti-Jesuit and inclined to sympathise with the Jansenists.

An English community in a foreign land had its share of difficulties, including two sieges of Douai. When Louis XIV entered the town in 1667 after a short siege, he attended Mass at St Gregory's; Downside still has a copy of the work against *commendam* which someone tactlessly placed on the king's prie-dieu before he arrived but which was fortunately retrieved in time by the Prior. In 1710 came another siege, this time by the English, and an interview was obtained with Marlborough who ordered his batteries to avoid firing on the monastery. A detailed account of life in the school during the early eighteenth century survives from the pen of a boy who entered in 1721. Gilbert Langley travelled from London with Prior Stourton and compared the community's welcome of the

Prior on his return, not very happily, to Milton's description of 'Lucifer's return to his fallen angels, which it so nearly resembled'. Langley had been a day-boy at the Charterhouse and found the academic standards of his new school much more exacting. He described a midnight kitchen raid in which he took part with five other boys, including a nephew of the poet Pope, and which led to a pitched battle with the French servants. Jacobite sympathies survived in the community and among their brethren of St Edmund's, in Paris, where James II was buried. A monk of St Gregory's, Michael Ellis, was consecrated Bishop in London at James II's chapel royal, but ended his days after the Revolution of 1688 as a popular and energetic Bishop of Segni in the Campagna. Bishop Ellis was a son of an Anglican clergyman. His eldest brother was a Secretary of State of William III, a second filled a similar office for the exiled James II, while a third was the Protestant Bishop of Meath. Another Benedictine bishop had friendly relations with the Hanoverian Government. This was Charles Walmesley, a pupil of the school at Douai who became a monk of St Edmund's, Paris, and succeeded as Vicar Apostolic of the Western District in 1764. As a well-known astronomer and mathematician, he was elected a Fellow of the Royal Society and advised the English Government on the adoption of the Gregorian Calendar.

The outbreak of the French Revolution brought nearly two centuries of history to an end. A few monks held on at Douai, hoping to save the buildings, but on the outbreak of war they were imprisoned at Doullens. The death of Robespierre brought an easing of their lot and they were transferred, still prisoners, back to their former home at Douai. They found the buildings plundered, the splendid library dispersed and the church ruined. Today manuscripts and books formerly belonging to the monastic library can be found in the town libraries of Douai, Lille and Arras. A wing of the former monastery survives, completed in 1781, and embedded in the buildings of a *lycée*,

while the street in which it stands is still named rue de St
Benoît. One wonders what the French pupils make of the
memorial tablets of English monks in the cloister. At this
low point in the fortunes of the community a former pupil
of the school came to its rescue. Sir Edward Smythe, the
fifth baronet of Acton Burnell in Shropshire, had entered
the school in 1770 following in the footsteps of his father
and grandfather. He built a wing on to his house and
sheltered the monks and boys at Acton Burnell until the
purchase of Downside in 1814. In that year, and again
after Waterloo, there were those who wished to return to
Douai. Fortunately the community decided to remain in
England and the Douai property was given to the revived
community of St Edmund's, whose monastery in Paris
had been destroyed in the Revolution.

By 1823 it was possible to begin building at Downside,
and seven years of steady expansion followed. The monks
had brought with them from Acton Burnell a learned
member of the former Maurist Congregation and a doctor
of the Sorbonne who guided the student monks in their
studies. No time was lost in attempting to replace the
library lost in the Revolution, and the course of reading
followed by the future Bishop Bernard Ullathorne is as
impressive in the 1830s as that of the young David
Knowles nearly a century later. Ullathorne read widely in
the Fathers: Augustine, Origen, Ambrose, Tertullian,
Chrysostom, but also in Bossuet and Pascal, and the more
modern philosophers. Clearly the uprooting of the Revolution had not destroyed the tradition of study and respect
for learning. Numbers in the school increased during these
years, rising from the seven who survived the Revolution
to sixty in 1830. At that point development was halted,
partly because of the system of government then obtaining
in the Congregation, which gave the President wide powers over the local communities. To him belonged the right
to withdraw monks from the monasteries to serve on the
many Benedictine missions scattered throughout the
country. This was a form of government that made it

impossible to build up large resident communities able to follow policies of their own making.

In a lecture to the British Academy of 1956 David Knowles described the Downside school entered by the young Aidan Gasquet in 1862:

> Downside was a small and stagnant school of some sixty boys of all ages from 12 to 18 ... staffed entirely by nine or ten monks all under thirty years of age. The boys came mostly from upper middle class homes, with a fair sprinkling of the old Catholic county families—Stourtons, Petres, Smythes, Throckmortons, Berkeleys, Vaughans, Fitzherberts—and a seasoning of the Irish landowning class; the monks themselves had almost without exception passed through the school, and there was consequently a family solidarity throughout school and monastery. The teaching was poor ... but a long tradition from the past and a succession of notable men, together with the possession of a library fairly strong in patristics and church history gave an atmosphere of breeding and culture of a peculiar cast but of very real power, and for some years at that time a young aristocrat of means [the 13th Lord Petre] acted as guide and philosopher to the senior boys and as fairy godmother to the community. The outlook was still that of a proud people aloof, and on the defensive. (Creighton Lecture: *Historian and Character*, 241)

There is some exaggeration in this passage and, judging by contemporary standards, the teaching was not perhaps so poor. For much of the nineteenth century the curriculum, as in most schools of its type, was mainly classical. In 1828, the year that saw Arnold begin his career at Rugby, the diary of a monk records the spare-time coaching he had given to a boy 'of no great abilities': during the school year they had covered the whole of Horace, three books of Livy, four satires of Juvenal, and some Terence. At Winchester, a school of less than seventy boys in 1860, the teaching of modern languages had hardly begun, although tentative efforts had been made in the 1850s when a German master shared a room with the school

hairdresser; at Downside, French, German and Italian
were already being taught in the 1840s. When Gasquet
entered the school in 1862 Catholics were excluded from
the ancient universities, but Downside had been affiliated
to the new London University in 1841, its boys began to
take the Matriculation examination, and soon young
monks were taking its external degrees.

By the time Gasquet was elected Prior, in 1878, a new
and fruitful phase had opened. The new Prior, himself
only thirty-two years of age, found himself at the head of a
small community of some thirteen monks, but it included
a group of unusually able young men. They had far-
reaching hopes for the future of both monastery and
school, ambitious plans indeed, marked by the scrapping
of foundations prepared for a new church and the building
of the transept of a great monastic church which would
eventually compare in size with the neighbouring
cathedral at Wells. Laymasters were introduced into the
school and scholarly interests were stimulated by frequent
visits from the liturgist, Edmund Bishop, himself a
polymath. The community soon moved into one of the
new buildings, a spacious monastery which would house
fifty or more monks. Yet a talented community had little
control over its destinies; the demands of the parishes
came first.

Inevitably a movement for constitutional reform began,
and Downside pressure induced the friendly diocesan
Bishop Clifford to petition the Holy See in 1880 for an
investigation into the form of government of the English
Benedictine Congregation. In his remarkable account of
Abbot Butler, reprinted in the *Historian and Character*,
David Knowles gave an outline of the constitutional
struggle that ensued, tenaciously opposed by older members of the Congregation and its governing body, aided by
the traditional delays of the Roman authorities. Twenty
years passed before final success was achieved with the
erection of the individual monasteries as autonomous
abbeys. Downside could now plan its own future, and an

early result was the fostering of higher studies. By 1894 a small group of monks, including Gasquet and Cuthbert Butler, were living with Edmund Bishop in a house near the British Museum, engaged on historical research. Two years later a house was opened at Cambridge where monks could study as members of Christ's College. It was not long before the University Press had published works of distinction produced by its members, and Dom Hugh Connolly became a member of the Board of Oriental Studies and a Tripos examiner. Notable progress in the school was delayed until the turn of the century and then marked by the election of the Headmaster to the Headmasters' Conference.

As Downside moved into the twentieth century there was much to give its community an assured confidence, proud still, perhaps, in the sense of the Knowles Creighton Lecture but no longer aloof or on the defensive. Consciousness of a tradition handed down through the centuries, the spiritual example of some outstanding men, an appreciation of scholarship, the possession of a great church, all these had their place. It was a very English community with the prejudices of its class, and national characteristics influenced the monks to share a somewhat condescending attitude to the fashionable theories of foreign monasticism which seemed exemplified at the time in the German Congregation of Beuron. Having fought so hard for its own autonomy the community would be always suspicious of foreign belief in the advantages of centralisation. From the seventeenth century St Gregory's had numbered among its monks the occasional convert from the Anglican Church but the converts of the Oxford Movement had passed it by. From 1922 onwards Downside was to be governed by three distinguished Abbots who had been ordained in the Church of England. It was perhaps through this influence, added to a distaste for religious controversy, that Downside was found sympathetic not only by Catholic writers and scholars such as Baron von Hügel, but by many Anglican visitors. It came to exercise an ecumenical·influence long before that word had become part of the modern ecclesiastical vocabulary. The year 1914 seemed to mark a climax of three centuries of Gregorian history with the elevation of Dom Aidan Gasquet to the cardinalate. This was the year when David Knowles entered the novitiate.

Chapter Two

ET IN ARCADIA

The school at Downside had its deep lovers (*et in Arcadia ego*) in those days.

D. K to A. M., 1974

Michael Clive Knowles, generally known by his name in religion of David, was born on 29 September 1896, in the closing years of the Victorian age. It was a year before the Queen's second Jubilee, and the certainties and complacencies of the age were at their height. A growing population was reaching a degree of economic prosperity hitherto unknown and a self-confident imperialism found political expression in the *imperium et libertas* of Disraeli and a literary voice in the writings of Rudyard Kipling that in time would influence the young Knowles. Already in this year of his birth had occurred the Jameson Raid which pointed the way to the Boer War, and three years earlier the Independent Labour Party had been formed at Bradford. These were forces destined to move the country away from the self-confidence of the Victorians and reach fruition in the boy's lifetime.

The child's background on both sides of his family was typical of the period and its virtues, with grandparents on both sides of nonconformist religion, who had made their way by intelligence and industry to positions of some affluence. In 1850 his maternal great-grandfather had founded the firm of William Hall and Company, makers of

needles and pins and later of all the gramophone needles
for His Master's Voice. This was inherited by his daughter and her husband, a Londoner named John Morgan.
David's mother was a member of their large family and
spent her childhood in the Queen Anne manor house of
the Warwickshire village of Studley, which was later to be
David's own home for some years. Family tradition had it
that the Knowles family had been a landowning family of
North-east Warwickshire that had fallen in the social
scale; they were descended from the Holt family, holders
of Aston Hall for the king during the Civil War. David's
paternal grandfather was a Birmingham timber merchant
and something of a character, born in the era of the
stagecoach in 1823 and just missing the First World War
by dying in 1912. The Morgans were Baptist and the
Knowles were Congregationalists. Both families took their
religion seriously and adhered to the strict Sunday régime
of nineteenth-century nonconformity.

   David's father Harry was born in 1865 and in time
became a partner in the Hall firm as a result of a school
friendship with the younger John Morgan. This led eventually to marriage with John's sister Carrie. He was a
young man of wide interests, a lover of the countryside
and widely read, indeed it was his reading of Newman
that led him to break away from his rigid nonconformist
background and end as a member of the Church of Rome.
David was always conscious of the intellectual debt he
owed to his father and, until 1939, their relationship was
unusually close. To him he owed his interest in the folk-
lore of the countryside, his interest in cricket, and his first
reading of the works of Walter Scott. An estrangement
came between them at the end of his father's life, but when
he died David wrote of him: 'I remember him chiefly for
his goodness and love—and ... for his mind. In my
judgements and tastes I owe more than I can say to
him ... As a person he reminded me more of Sir Thomas
More (in his personal relations) than any other.' David's
mother seems to have influenced him less, partly because

of her frail health. She was skilled in the arts thought suitable for a young Victorian girl, was musical and an excellent hostess. Both parents had a fund of affection and care to spend for others, and a strong and pervading religious faith.

David was their only surviving child and was baptised a Catholic although at the time his father was still under instruction and his mother had not yet decided to follow him into the Roman Catholic Church. From the age of five he accompanied his father on Sundays to Mass at Coughton Court, two miles from Studley. Coughton was the seat of an old Catholic family, the Throckmortons, many of whom had been educated at Downside, and after Catholic Emancipation in 1829 they had built a stone church and priest's house for the local congregation. In time, a group of Warwickshire parishes developed from Coughton, all served by Benedictine monks of Douai Abbey. It was of some significance for his future that the district round David's home was ministered to by Benedictines. The family home at Studley and later at Alcester was always open to the parish priest, and David came to know several of them very well, especially Dom Bede Ryan, who was typical of the Douai monk of that age: a lover of the liturgy, well read, kindly, with an enthusiasm for cricket.

Childhood was a happy and sheltered time, but in some ways a lonely one, for Studley provided no boy friends of his own age. A welcome companionship over two years was provided by a cousin, Margaret Loxton, the daughter of a Knowles aunt. She came to share his nurse and first governess and a lifelong friendship resulted, a bond which was strengthened when Margaret became a Catholic and in time joined the Benedictine nuns of Stanbrook Abbey, Worcester. In 1904 the family moved to Alcester taking an interesting seventeenth-century house with a garden bounded by the River Arrow. There was plenty of interest here for a normal boy, and the river could be explored with the help of an aged punt and paddles. David came to know this shallow stream in all its seasons, bathing in

summer and floating on summer evenings with his father
in the punt by candlelight.

School did not break into this pleasant existence until
David was ten years old, probably because he was
regarded as a delicate child and his parents were over-
protective. In 1906 he entered West House School at Edg-
baston, first as a day-boy and later as a weekly boarder. It
was a transition which could not have been easy. A succession of governesses had done little to provide a solid
educational foundation, his childhood had been spent
mostly alone, and he had never been summoned by bells,
or played the usual school games. In time he developed
interests that compensated for the trials of school life. An
enthusiasm for railways lasted all his life; he studied *Bradshaw* and the *Railway Magazine* and acquired a knowledge
of the many different lines. Later he was to add a line, now
gone, which has lingered in the memory of many monks
and boys of Downside. This was the Somerset and Dorset
line that ran from Bath to Templecombe and was known
affectionately to its clients as 'The Slow and Dirty'. In
days gone the driver would hold his train beyond the
appointed time at Chilcompton if he saw the Downside
car descending the slope to the station. Members of the
community, like the Duke of Beaufort at Badminton, were
privileged to ask the guard at Bath to stop a fast train for
them. Time spent waiting for trains was never for David a
matter for irritation or boredom. He could spend an hour
or so happily watching the international expresses thun-
dering through the station at Dijon, and he is recorded by
Professor Brooke as enjoying any delay, even at Bletchley,
a name of ill omen to many travellers from Oxford or
Cambridge University. *Wisden* also became a favourite
study, and David was a devoted supporter of the county
team. In his last summer term he secured a place in the
school XI and it was through cricket that he made his first
enduring school friendship with a boy whose father, Col-
onel Martineau, was later Lord Mayor of Birmingham.
Gaston Martineau went on to Rugby, but the two boys

kept in touch and met during school holidays. When Gaston died in 1973 David wrote to his Stanbrook cousin asking for prayers for him: 'He was 100% good but (so far as I know) quite without Christian faith—and as a cradle-Unitarian I doubt whether he had been baptised.' David recalled that both, as non-members of the Anglican Church, had been exempted from school prayers. This last summer term was a happy one and ended with the news that he had been awarded a scholarship to Downside School.

David entered Downside School in 1910 at an interesting time when it was undergoing transformation at the hands of a great Headmaster who had been appointed in 1902. Dom Leander Ramsay was a convert from Anglicanism and had been Vice-Principal of the neighbouring theological college at Wells, an Oxford man with an admiration for the public-school tradition. As a boy of fourteen David was impressed by him at their first meeting and to the end of his life regarded him as the one really great man he had ever known at all intimately. The Headmaster was indeed an exceptional man, an established patristic scholar but also a practical administrator of great determination.

A monastic school controlled by a community, most of whose members were former pupils, risks being inbred and inward looking. Ramsay with his Oxford and Anglican background brought fresh vision to bear on old traditions, instituting wide-ranging reforms in the school which did not always meet with unanimous approval at the time. He swept away a framework which had remained largely unchanged for three centuries and the rewards were great. Before long other old-established Catholic schools followed where he had led. As Headmaster he had his limitations and was not endowed with any special understanding of boys. One member of his staff, Dom Lucius Graham, once remarked that the Headmaster was the worst judge of character in Christendom, but he added that, when one was most infuriated by his actions, it was a consolation to reflect that one was being driven to distraction by a great man. Through all the success of these years the Headmaster showed a complete lack of self-interest in his aims and judgements. The boys might see him in church completely absorbed in prayer; in later days as Abbot his monks were conscious of his utter gift of recollection as he stood in the cloister *statio* while the bells rang for Office, or in his stall in choir.

Dom Leander remained somewhat in the background as Headmaster and, as the school was organised in 1910, the monk who had the most immediate impact on the boys was Dom Wulstan Pearson. He was then under forty years of age and formed a complete contrast to the ex-Anglican Headmaster, having been educated at Douai in France—a sound disciplinarian and judge of boys. He was also a cricketer of some standing who had been invited, and declined, to keep wicket for Somerset. Corporal punishment was not missing from his régime and formed part of the powers then wielded by the Head Boy and the two Captains of games. In the case of Dom Wulstan it was administered with complete impartiality, was never a cause for grudge, and the boys as a whole appreciated his care for each individual. He was to become in turn the Prior of Ealing and the first Bishop of Lancaster. In Ramsay and Pearson the Downside boy of that time came under the influence of two remarkable men who complemented each other, but it may be added that Dom Wulstan had no appreciation of or sympathy for Dom Leander's extensive reforms.

During his first year David was taught by monks and by laymasters, and the memory of a few of these still survives. Dom Peter Worsley-Worswick, member of an old Catholic landowning family, was a man of culture, of gentle personality and an indefatigable cross-country walker. Those who knew him at a later time and were affectionately amused by his idiosyncracies found it difficult to realise that he had ever taken part in the training of boys. A much more definite personality was Dom Lucius Graham, who was to survive on the teaching staff over a long period. He was a most effective and stimulating teacher of his subjects, English and History. Gifted with an unusually retentive memory he could quote pages of the Shakespeare plays by heart and he could produce the memorable phrase that lingered in the minds of pupils long after they had left school. He believed in revision for the examinations of the Oxford and Cambridge Board: on summer evenings a large voluntary audience attended revision classes in the Gasquet Hall, attired in pyjamas and dressing-gowns, and a last run-through was given in the examination hall before the papers were opened. His uncanny knack on these occasions of rehearsing questions which came in the paper persuaded some of his pupils that he had taken a prior look at the questions set, which in fact was not the case. Dom Lucius was a shrewd but kindly judge of character, and the possessor of a sharp wit greatly relished both by the boys and his brethren.

Later in his school life David encountered Dom Roger Hudleston, a convert to the Church and a man of many talents. He could surprise one by a passing reference to an experience in Tiflis Cathedral or display a detailed knowledge of manuscripts of the medieval English mystics. He edited a series of spiritual classics known as the Orchard series, but also under the pseudonym of Roger Pater published volumes of strange stories of the supernatural. It was then the custom for a sermon to be preached on Sundays at the Mass in the Abbey church which was attended by the school, and the preacher had the difficult task of producing a discourse suitable for two critical audiences, boys and monks. Two preachers of this time were outstanding in their entertainment value, and of these Dom Roger was the star. His delivery was dramatic, with an excessive emphasis on the syllables, and one phrase passed into the community folk-lore, the picture of an asylum with its 'hoary dotards building castellas in the mudda'. It was a thrilling Sunday for the boys when they saw the Master of Ceremonies lead Dom Roger from his choir stall

to the pulpit, an experience not unlike that of the crowd
which greeted C. B. Fry when he emerged from the pavi-
lion at a county match. One other performance was long
remembered: Dom Roger's rendering of the first Lamenta-
tion at *Tenebrae*. The writer of these pages came too late to
experience it but, many years after David first heard it, Sir
Richard Sykes achieved some renown by his excellent
imitation of the original artist.

Among the laymasters of this time one especially was
remembered with delight by many generations of Downside boys. He was a science graduate of Bristol University
and a somewhat unusual member of the lay staff in that
respect. But he was an excellent teacher, given to making
the occasional joke which produced from his audience the
'Lush Roar'. This could be heard from afar and caused
anguish to masters taking neighbouring classes, as the
volume of noise was not commensurate with the wit that
produced it. The 'Lush Roar' was somehow tolerated
by the authorities and remained a feature of Downside
science until its producer retired in 1939.

The boys of West House had all come from an identical
background, that of the professional classes of Birmingham, and Downside provided a richly varied selection of
schoolfellows. The old Catholic families traditionally connected with the school provided their contingent, and its
growing reputation brought sons and grandsons of converts to the Church, sons of diplomats, barristers, men of
letters. There was a strong contingent of county families
from Ireland, and an unusual element was provided by a
few boys from the great historical Polish families: Czar-
toryski, Sapieha, Potocki. For some reason the Headmaster refused to admit foreign boys, but one Polish boy
had earlier gained admission and by his charm had
smoothed the way for others. They were to remain a successful element until the Second World War, and when it
ended a Sapieha and a Zamoyski appeared again on the
school lists. Among David's contemporaries were a few of
the usual school eccentrics, including the Irish boy who

poured mercury into the ear of a chemistry master as he
bent down to observe an experiment.

The most remarkable of these was Osmund Grattan
Esmonde, eldest son of an Irish baronet, who chose to play
the part of a patriarch of the Orthodox Church. Dressed
for the part in flowing robes and the black brimless hat
made familiar in modern times by Archbishop Makarios
he managed to secure a ride on the footplate of a Somerset
and Dorset engine to the mystification of its crew. Two
other boys added more than most to the gaiety of school
life. Cyril Riccardi-Cubitt was a descendant on his father's
side of the builder of Pimlico and through his mother, last
of the Florentine Riccardi, heir to an Italian title. He was
something of a rebel, ingenious with plans for enlivening
the daily round, with a credulous victim in Ian Chesney
who also had an unusual background, having spent his
prep-school days in Lausanne.

The first term passed quickly with all its new experi-
ences, and David left for home by horse brake to Chilcompton, where two special trains were waiting, one
bound for London and the other for the North. The
Christmas holidays brought a minor disaster. His
enthusiasm for trains had made him a welcome visitor at
his local station and one night he fell in the engine shed
and badly damaged a knee. Return to school was impossible, and for a new boy to miss his second term is a real
misfortune. David lost a term's work and the gap in his
basic knowledge was never quite made good, in addition
to which he also lost discipline and companionship at an
important point in his life at school. In the summer term
he was unable to play cricket at which, as a member of his
prep-school XI, he might have shone. By the end of his
first year he had found school life frustrating and disap-
pointing.

A lift to his spirits came when he returned to school in
September and found that he had been given a study of his
own. It was one of nine which were known as the Attics,
reached by a turret stone staircase from the Court of

Arches. It was small, with barely more space than allowed for a bed, a desk, and bookshelves, cold in winter and hot in summer. The Attics were rather remote from the main life of the school and the nine members tended to form a tight little community of their own. They came to know one another extremely well, and here for David was a new experience which helped to transform his attitude to school life. Among the nine was a Scot, Jimmy Coats, the eldest son of a wealthy cotton baronet; Dermot Browne, second son of the Earl of Kenmare; Mervyn and Roy Pontifex, sons of a convert Anglican clergyman; Geoffrey Snead-Cox, son of an author and journalist; and Gervase de Bless whose mother was a sister of the well-known singer, Gervase Elwes. Only one of these nine boys had a father who was not a convert to the Church, and as a group they formed a great contrast to the boys he had known at West House. In one of them especially he found someone reflecting all the cultural tastes to which he was drawn but had hitherto missed.

Gervase de Bless, albeit without knowing, had a strong influence on the young Knowles. He was the son of a barrister and a mother who was a member of an old Lincolnshire family living partly at Billing Hall near Northampton and partly in the manor house at Brigg. These were owned by his uncle, Gervase Elwes, a one time diplomat, now a landowner and notable singer, who had married Lady Winefride Feilding, daughter of a convert parent, the Earl of Denbigh. The Elwes were devout Catholics with a private chapel and daily Mass, and it was in this atmosphere that Gervase de Bless had grown up at Billing. He had travelled extensively with his parents and had acquired an appreciation of great art, architecture and music. For a boy of his age he had read fairly widely, had a keen interest in cricket, and above all in fishing. His fishing diaries, now at Downside, record his exploits on the Test and other rivers, and contain the comment that, whereas fishing was regarded as beyond contempt and forbidden at most public schools, at Downside it was considered by the authorities to be a harmless, if eccentric, activity. He was a gifted and unusual boy and popular with his contemporaries. One result of his influence was David's increased interest in his religion. It was at this time that he became a daily communicant.

In a school which then numbered some two hundred boys it was still possible for something of a family spirit to prevail, and a traditional religious framework to be observed which has disappeared to some extent with the modern belief that the practice of religion by the young is best conducted on a voluntary basis. All new boys learnt to serve Mass which all attended daily; there were prayers before classes and recitation of the mid-day *Angelus*. Holy Week brought an interruption of the normal school routine and classes were suspended for two days while the boys made a brief Retreat that helped to an understanding of the liturgy. Music in the Abbey church followed a tradition established by Sir Richard Terry, a balance of plain-song sung by the monks and of polyphony sung by the school choir, the music of Byrd, Palestrina, and Vitoria, with responses at *Tenebrae* sung to the fine setting of Ingegneri with the *Jerusalem* of Tallis. The nave of the Abbey church had not yet been built but the setting was one of beauty, likely to make a great impression on a sensitive boy. David also joined a group of boys who chose to attend the Sunday evening service of sung Compline. It was sung by the monks to a simple Gregorian chant at dusk in summer and in darkness during the winter, save for the light of two candles on the altar. At its end the monks moved off in procession from the choir to the Lady Chapel where they sang the antiphon, and then left one by one with raised hoods as the *summum silentium*, or great silence, began. This was a short service which all visitors found impressive in a way that its vernacular replacement cannot equal. His awareness of this life of prayer, following its daily round independently of the school, began to inspire in David a desire to share it when the time came to choose his future life.

In 1912 the completion of spacious new buildings made possible the adoption of a modified House system and brought David into contact with the new Housemaster of Caverel, Dom Sigebert Trafford. Dom Sigebert was a member of an old Norfolk family and a nephew of a great benefactor of Downside, the thirteenth Lord Petre. It was after some masterful action of his that Dom Lucius Graham commented that it was typical of a family which had been bawling at gamekeepers for a thousand years. His was a remarkable personality, and calm and friendly relationships might be followed by sudden disciplinary activity when offending garments left about in the dormitories might be flung through the windows on to the lawns outside. Such occasions were known to the rest of the school as 'gala nights in Caverel'. If high handed and unpredictable Dom Sigebert had great charm and was never at a loss. Some years later when he was Headmaster he arrived at the Pump Room Hotel in Bath for dinner with the 1st XV on a day when there was a congress of Anglican clergy. To his surprise he was greeted as an old friend by a high Anglican dignitary who remarked: 'Well Canon, I see you haven't brought the old Archdeacon along this time, how is he these days?' 'Getting along you know, getting along,' came Dom Sigebert's immediate reply, 'of course not as young as he used to be; and we all thought that what with his chest and these fogs it might be wiser not to risk it. I'll tell him you asked.' There was the occasion during the war when he told me to accompany him to a London meeting presided over by the Archbishop of Canterbury. I had not been invited and felt somewhat ill at ease when we took seats on the front row of the platform close to the Archbishop. My uneasiness increased when an important-looking clergyman in uniform arrived and enquired of Abbot Trafford: 'I am His Majesty's Chaplain-General to the Forces, can you tell me where I am seated?' Waving a hand over his shoulder the Abbot replied: 'Somewhere at the back I imagine, somewhere at the back.'

David was also now a pupil of a new member of the lay staff, Nevile Watts. Nevile was the son of an Anglican clergyman, a fairly recent convert to the Roman Catholic Church, and a former scholar of Peterhouse at Cambridge, who had achieved a First in the Classical Tripos. He became a part of the Downside scene and his sons later made their mark in the school. Hugh, a Cambridge Captain of Cricket, was to be supervised by David at Peterhouse. Nevile's enthusiasms were to inspire many of his pupils, not only for classical literature but also for his favourite Milton and Matthew Arnold. Long walks across the Mendips, ending with tea in his rooms, became a regular part of school life.

A surviving contemporary of David has recorded some impressions of his life during the last two years at school when he was a member of the classical sixth form. He played cricket with enthusiasm, if without great skill, and enjoyed an occasional morning net with the ex-Yorkshire professional. Today the cricket field at Downside is doubled in size but is still distractingly beautiful to a player in the way that the playing-fields of St John's can be along the Cambridge Backs. Below lie the school buildings dominated by the Abbey church and beyond, a distant view to the hills above Bath. There were cycle rides on summer evenings and visits to the fine Mendip churches: Mells, Leigh-on-Mendip, Chewton Mendip and Bruton. There were whole holidays when a party cycled to Bath to spend a day on the Avon, and an occasion when one of the party was overcome by the cider drunk at lunch. In the current jargon derived from their study of Euripides's *Bacchae:* 'the god had him'. A group of six made these expeditions in wet weather or fine, to Glastonbury on a wet Whit Monday with a change into dry clothing and lunch at the George Inn, and a visit to Cheddar in the strawberry season at a time when a procession of cars had not destroyed the impact of a descent through the Gorge.

Near the end of the last war it was the writer's good fortune to travel up the Cheddar Gorge on a moonlight night in an American Army Jeep, returning from a prisoner-of-war camp near Bristol. The complete absence of other traffic and the heavy silence of a summer night brought a sense of travelling up an alpine valley, round sharp turns with the limestone cliff rising higher at each point. David's generation was perhaps the last to see the Mendip country utterly unspoilt, and he never lost his early love of it, with its sudden hills and unexpected valleys. During his final year he began to write a school novel. Ten years later I was allowed to read the two chapters he had completed and I may have been the only one permitted to read them. The plot, I remember, had not yet unfolded for the story had barely proceeded beyond what the old-fashioned writers on meditation would have termed 'composition of place'. I was impressed at the time by David's description of the Mendip country in winter, with its echo of Emily Bronte's description of another countryside in *Wuthering Heights:*

> There was a hint of desolation in some of the upland pastures in winter, with sycamores and beeches bare in October and trees warped towards the northeast by the prevailing sou'westers that crept up from the Atlantic beyond Exmoor, but again and again as one walked there came a sudden drop from a stone-walled field to a deep flooded combe with a stream breaking from the limestone. In places one could stand on a crag at the summit of a steep hillside almost on air and watch the valley below.

This was a remarkably sensitive piece of writing for a boy of seventeen and foreshadowed the historian's style. One can only wonder what sort of book would have resulted had David persevered. In 1972 he recalled the Downside of this time and the Warwickshire of his childhood in a letter to Abbot Trafford:

> Downside was a manageable place, with buildings kept in check by lawns and trees, a village of village size with no fast and heavy through traffic. How I would enjoy a holiday in

the Warwickshire of my childhood of horse traffic, unlighted
roads, three fords to the mile in the lanes, and villagers who
had never been 20 miles from home in their lives.

When David was a schoolboy the Mendip villages had
changed little since the Crimean War. In recent times one
of the Abbey carpenters recalled that in those days his
grandfather, who had worked for the monks since 1814,
was the only local man able to read and write. He had sat
on a chair in the village square every Sunday to read news
of the war to the villagers from a Sunday newspaper. A
school conducted by the Servite nuns was soon to provide
literacy but in other respects time had stood still.

Among David's contemporaries were some very
talented boys. Ivone Kirkpatrick, whose mother had at
one time been a Maid of Honour to Queen Victoria,
became a distinguished diplomat and Permanent Head of
the Foreign Office. Dick Stokes, the dynamic Head boy,
became a rugger blue and won a Military Cross in the
First World War, with a seat in Parliament later as Downside's first Labour member. He became an unconven-
tional Minister of the Crown who once startled his civil
servants by removing his trousers to dry them on a wet
morning and sat without them throughout a conference.
Douglas Woodruff became President of the Oxford Union
and a distinguished journalist and author. Two contemporaries died in the war: Prince Alfred Sapieha fought in
the Austrian army and wrote to David one of his last
letters from the Russian front; Gervase de Bless died as a
midshipman in the Royal Navy.

It was David's relations with Gervase de Bless that cast
a shadow over the final school year. He had been strongly
attracted and impressed by him, and their walks and discussions had revealed a fascinating world of foreign travel,
of visits to the Uffizi and San Marco, and to the opera at
La Scala and Bayreuth. Yet companionship had not
grown into intimate friendship. Gervase de Bless had been
disappointed in one close school friendship and had re-

solved to form no more, but David was unwilling to be
satisfied with their normal companionship. He developed
a love-hate attitude to this boy and finally a silence fell
between them; he decided to sever relations and during
the last months of his school career David met Gervase de
Bless daily in class and elsewhere but never spoke to him
again. The episode has some relevance to an understanding of the man whose later development was to be so
unexpected.

David's school file confirms that this was a period of
stress. A note to the Headmaster complains of poor class
work and of indiscipline; a letter from his father reveals
that the family doctor was concerned about his health. He
had had his share of success in examinations, with distinctions in English and Roman History in the Higher
Certificate; he had edited the school magazine, *The Raven*,
but in a fit of depression resigned his office. He had not,
however, surprisingly, shown real brilliance and was not
regarded as a potential university scholar; he had made no
mark at school games and had been passed over as Head
of his House. If David had become a rather troublesome
sixth-form boy at this time he was himself conscious of a
sense of failure. Something of this appeared in a letter he
wrote to me in 1929:

> I think in so many ways you have been too lucky; things have
> been too easy for you . . . It was my fortune to fail in every-
> thing for the first five years of my religious life and most of my
> school life—fail to get everything I wanted, especially friend-
> ship.

The end of the school year of 1914 was marked by a
great local celebration. A century had passed since the
monks had first come to Downside after expulsion from
revolutionary France and the stay of twenty years at
Acton Burnell Hall, home of their old pupil Sir Edward
Smythe. That in itself was worthy of celebration but it so
happened that this summer saw the elevation of Abbot

Gasquet to the cardinalate and the succession of Abbot Cuthbert Butler as President of the English Benedictine Congregation. A large and distinguished company assembled to receive the new Cardinal. A gift of splendid cloth-of-gold vestments, woven in Moscow, had been made for use at the pontifical Mass, celebrated in the presence of all the Roman Catholic bishops. There was a reception and a cricket match. It was an occasion for what today would be called triumphalism, or more sensibly the thanksgiving for a century of great achievement, and it reflected the confidence and security of the pre-war society. A threat unrealised hung over the gathering. Within a month some of David's contemporaries were offering themselves for the Services; of seven principal performers in a school play only two were to survive the war. For the Headmaster it was to seem that the living work of years was destined to destruction.

Chapter Three

THE YOUNG MONK

There was a wild cherry by the woodside at Luccombe
pond that I could see from the window of my cell, and
that I looked for every year.

D. K. to A. M.

For some years David had looked forward to the day when
he would join the community. He had felt a vocation to be
a priest but not a call to a particular ministry and was
drawn by the thought of a life centred on God and by a
love of the liturgy. He was barely eighteen years old.
Today we tend to delay the admission of novices until
their university course is completed, to deprecate the
admission of boys direct from school, and after completion
of a novitiate to delay for several years the day when they
commit themselves by solemn vows. A different tradition
obtained in 1914, and at no time did David ever regret his
early decision. It was always his view that a delay of three
or four years and a more mature judgement would not
have made for greater wisdom of choice. His last summer
holiday was spent while the Battle of the Marne was being
fought in France, and at the end of September he took
farewell of his parents and returned to Downside, no
longer a schoolboy. He was under military age and few
believed at that time that the war would last long.

The novitiate at Downside dated from 1908 when
Abbot Cuthbert Butler, not without disapproval from

28

other houses of the Congregation, had withdrawn his young monks from the common novitiate which had been established at Belmont, near Hereford, in 1859. Life at Belmont had been extremely austere and the novice masters had not necessarily been Downside monks, several of the more distinguished ones having been supplied by Ampleforth and Douai. Removal of the novices to Downside inevitably brought with it not only a break with the immediate past but a difference in outlook between older monks trained at Belmont and a younger section influenced since 1908 by Abbot Butler. The 1908 novitiate had been a large one, and six of its members had taken vows. Two of them, Ambrose Agius and Rupert Hall, were remembered as outstanding games players while in the school, Alphege Shebbeare was a musician convert from Anglicanism, Thomas Symons was also a musician, and Anselm Rutherford an ex-Anglican member of King's College, Cambridge. Their arrival had coincided with the introduction of Solesmes plain-chant and much liturgical development, and somehow they had acquired the nickname of the 'Usques', from a phrase used of the Congregation in a recent papal Bull: *'usquequaque monastica'* or 'wholly monastic'. The name implied a certain austerity of outlook compared with that of the generation which preceded them. Gradually David and his fellow novice, Mark Pontifex, came into contact with these and other young monks previously unknown to them in the school.

A group senior to the 'Usques' had in its turn reacted from the archaic atmosphere of mid-nineteenth-century Catholicism, and some of them had passed through the school in their day while others were converts to the Church with a background of the Anglican public schools. Among them were Bruno Hicks, Sigebert Trafford, and Austin Corney; others included Urban Butler, who was the cultured son of a well-known Victorian artist, Lady Butler, and had a military family background; Raymond Webster who came from Harrow and New College, Oxford, was something of an expert on Byzantine and art

history and later rendered great service as monastic librarian. Paul Brookfield was the son of Charles Brookfield,
actor and playwright, and his literary wife. These formed
a lighthearted contrast to the younger and more serious
'Usques'.

Contacts with all of these were, however, few, and during the first year of the novitiate the young men were
almost completely segregated from the community, meeting them only briefly on Sundays and Feastdays after
dinner. Much therefore depended on the novice master,
and in a large novitiate the companionship of others could
promote relief and amusement. Owing to the war David
and Br Mark missed much of this companionship. My
own memories of the novitiate are associated with laughter; cheerfulness kept breaking in, and there were times
when some among us were ordered by the novice master
to leave the refectory for yielding to the excessive laughter
which St Benedict commanded his monks to avoid. At this
time the novitiate contained only three who were senior to
David and Mark: Aidan Trafford, a younger brother of
Dom Sigebert; Meinrad Bertie, a younger brother of the
Earl of Abingdon whose sister had married Aidan Trafford's eldest brother; and Sylvester Hurlstone-Jones of
Magdalen College, Oxford, a convert from Anglicanism
and an artist of some merit. Aidan Trafford was perhaps
the liveliest and was possessed of charm and humour,
sporting tastes, and the ability to get his own way. He was
to show great kindness and act as a wise mentor many
years later when I became the youngest Housemaster in
the school.

David's novice master was Dom Wilfred Corney who
had at one time spent a number of years in Rome as
Procurator of the English Benedictine Congregation. He
was loved by all who knew him, was very devout and
almost too kindly and unworldly. When I came to know
him it was difficult to imagine him showing his novices the
dura et aspera emphasised by St Benedict in the Rule, a fault
of which I could not accuse my own novice master. The

novices were also in daily contact with Dom Laurence
Kynaston, who taught them classics and who was the son
of an Anglican clergyman and a descendant of Sir Robert
Peel. With Dom Laurence the novices read Aeschylus,
Homer and Theocritus, and from him David acquired an
early love of Wordsworth and Browning. As a young man
he had been an able games player but in later life he
planned and developed a magnificent alpine garden which
became widely known and drew expert gardeners from far
and wide. Stories about him were handed down in the
community for many years. With no ear for music he was
excused from the weekly choir practice after one at which
he had solemnly held an antiphonal upside down and
almost brought the practice to an abrupt end. He was an
excellent refectory reader with the ability to make a piece
of indifferent writing sound absurd without any change of
countenance. There was the dull book of medieval history
with its frequent mention of the place name Cobham,
invariably followed by the footnote 'or Chobham', and
each time this occurred Dom Laurence was able to express
heightened surprise which reduced his hearers to laughter.
He was a somewhat intimidating figure to a young man
for he did not suffer fools gladly, but David remembered
him always with affection and maintained that Dom
Laurence's knowledge of English literature approached
that of a Leavis or C. S. Lewis.

The novitiate period was a strenuous but happy one.
The day began at 4.30 am, and at 5 am David was in choir
for Mattins and Lauds, followed by an interval of a half
hour before returning to choir for Prime. After this came
mental prayer and the novitiate Mass. The sung conventual Mass was at 9 am, then the morning conference with
the novice master, the class in classics, with the main meal
of the day at 1.10 pm, after the brief choir Office of None.
Vespers were sung before supper which was at 7.30 pm,
and the last Office of the day, Compline, followed at 8.30
pm. Afternoons were usually given over to manual labour
in the open air and were mostly spent in thinning the

larches and pines which had been planted among the
beech trees to the north of the monastery, along the Mile
road, and in the College Wood. It was enjoyable work,
and the labourers had to learn how to swing a woodman's
axe. On windy and frosty days they appreciated the scent
and heat of the fires they kindled with lopped branches.
Later they learnt how to fell hardwoods, removing
diseased beeches with axe, cross-saw, wedges and ropes. A
later generation had the less interesting task of levelling an
extension of the upper cricket ground and worked in silence under the strict control of the novice master. In
summer, the novices were allowed an occasional game of
tennis and a bathe. This was essentially the novitiate
régime that lasted unchanged until after the Second
World War, physically demanding, monotonous and lacking much intellectual stimulus. Use of the monastic library was not permitted while newspapers and secular literature were banned.

One feature of the life of novices over a long period was
the twice-weekly Psalm class conducted by Dom Edmund
Kendal and remembered by many young monks as the
most tedious exercise of their week. Cheerful, kindly and
shy, the 'Doctor' was one of the more colourful members
of the community. Large in size, careless in dress, and
addicted to snuff, he was gifted with a powerful voice
which must surely have been predestined to be a source of
mortification to his brethren. Attempts to hide his *graduale*
or antiphonal were usually frustrated by his devotion to
the chant and willingness to sing by heart. I remember
noting with sympathy the distress once caused to that
sensitive musician, Dom Alphege Shebbeare, who found
himself next to Dom Edmund in choir when the latter was
moved to sing the *Salve Regina* fortissimo and off-key. Dom
Edmund was a model of observance and obedience and
therefore a natural candidate for the tasks no one else
wanted. The possession of a first-class mind did not prevent him from being a boring teacher, although he was
happily gifted with a tendency to slumber during his even-

ing classes. David once remarked that the 'Doctor' could never receive harsh treatment at the final judgement for his own charity was so profound, but on second thoughts he recalled the fury and frustration he had unwittingly caused to past pupils. He was moved to agony by Dom Edmund's dictation of notes and dull treatment of the Psalms. My own generation perhaps took things more lightly, and I remember Dom Edmund quitting our novices' class on occasion as a result of our lack of seriousness. Unknown to us he had another and unexpected activity—as a popular raconteur to the Junior House boys in the school. On wet afternoons they would find a monk to act as their messenger and beg Dom Edmund to come down and entertain them with his stories. Once ensconced in their Day Room he would be besieged with requests: 'O Sir, tell us the one about how you walked the tight-rope over the waterfall. No, not that one. Please go on from where the dynamite was just going off and you were tied to a barrel of rum in the hold.'

During the first Christmas holidays classes ceased for a time and were replaced by a series of special conferences given by the Abbot, Dom Cuthbert Butler. When Benet House was established in Cambridge in 1896 he had been chosen as its first Head, and his editions of the Lausiac History of Palladius and of the Rule of St Benedict had gained him a reputation as a scholar of distinction. Ten years later he had been elected Abbot and his spirituality, his reputation for learning, his clear vision of the aims of a monastic community, made him an inspiring leader. When Abbot Butler died in 1934 David published a brilliant memoir of him which did ample justice to his qualities as monk and scholar, and to his remarkable personality. He emphasised Abbot Butler's 'powerful and essentially masculine mind' and mentioned lighter aspects: the Abbot's appearance as he sallied forth for an afternoon's manual labour, clad in ancient garments, of which he observed that even so clad the mental power and distinction that was present in every line of Abbot Butler's countenance made it impossible for him to have passed for an ordinary man. He also mentioned the two undergraduates who engaged in a competition of telling anecdotes to the Abbot, the winner being the one who told the greater number of proved excellence which were not appreciated. But David summed up Abbot Butler's qualities as a religious superior:

> His distinguished appearance and reputation for learning, together with a certain aloofness of manner which developed during his years of rule, could not fail to make an attitude of respect natural to those who came into contact with him. His clear grasp of principle and his still rarer gift of clear enunciation, at least on paper, helped him to rise above opportunism to statesmanship. His kindly nature and his deep piety were both evident to all his subjects, and could not fail to win their admiration.

Abbot Butler felt it was a duty to take a share in the formation of the novices, and it was through these Christmas conferences that David first came under his influence. He made a point in their course of introducing the novices to books that had deeply influenced his own spiritual life such as the *Confessions* of St Augustine, the *Fathers of the Desert*, the *Conferences of Cassian*, and some of the works of Newman. He read with them and commented on the seventeenth century writer Dom Augustine Baker, whose *Holy Wisdom* had had an important influence on generations of monks. In time David was himself to write on the teaching of Father Baker, and his opinions were to undergo some change of emphasis, but to the end he regarded *Holy Wisdom* as a formative book with only one superior, the *Ascent of Mount Carmel* of his favourite St John of the Cross.

At the end of the novitiate year David and Mark Pontifex made their simple profession for the three years that would bring them to the taking of solemn vows in 1918. They now began the two years of philosophy which formed part of the six-year course of study for the priesthood. The philosophy of those days would be unacceptable today with its formal courses in scholastic Logic, Ethics and Metaphysics, studied with the aid of a Latin textbook. The two Juniors were at least fortunate in their teacher, Dom Anselm Rutherford, who had studied in Rome some years earlier, after following a course of science at Cambridge. He was a stimulating teacher and a gifted mimic whose wit enlivened the daily classes. As sacristan and master of ceremonies he had brought his excellent taste to bear on the vestments and church furnishings with remarkable effect. In later years he was to fill the offices of Headmaster and Prior, and throughout his life was a model of a devout and observant monk. When the philosophy course came to an end and theology began, the inevitable 'Doctor' reappeared, and David found his classes as dull as those on the Psalms had been. Some relief, however, was found in the scripture classes of Dom Richard Davey, a much younger man, who had been trained at Sant' Anselmo and had recently returned from service as an army chaplain.

As a Junior, life was less restricted. After two years without ever spending a night away David and Mark Pontifex were permitted a brief stay at Belmont Abbey in 1916 and were able to meet some of their contemporaries from Belmont and Douai Abbey, Woolhampton. This gave them an opportunity to visit Malvern, where they met David's parents for lunch, the first meeting since he had entered the novitiate. A second short holiday was allowed in the following year and for the first time he became acquainted with the Carmelite nuns who lived in the old home of the Arundells at Lanherne in Cornwall. Their austere and enclosed life struck a responsive echo from David for he was beginning to have thoughts of a Carthusian life of seclusion in the Charterhouse. At this stage this was not felt as dissatisfaction with the life at Downside, but as a desire to give himself more completely to God in a life severed from all human ties. Such ideas enter the minds of novices from time to time and do not last.

David claimed that for the next twelve years the hope remained that in time he might be privileged to lead a Carthusian life. If so, this was entirely unsuspected by his intimate friends in the community, and he did not show by external signs that this was the direction to which his hopes tended.

It was now permitted to use the monastic library, although the daily routine did not allow much time for private reading. Today the library is housed in a fine modern building, but at that time it was scattered over a number of rooms in the monastery and along the church cloister. It was a formidable collection, enriched by the bequest of Edmund Bishop's historical and liturgical books, with a wealth of periodicals and standard works, especially in history, art, classics and theology. Despite lack of time the amount of reading which David covered was truly remarkable, indeed few university undergraduates today would manage to accomplish so much outside their chosen field. He began, unsystematically, to read the masterpieces of English literature and history, using odd periods of free time. In this way he worked through the poets—Milton, Wordsworth, Tennyson and Browning and much of Keats and Shelley. In an address to a congress of historians in 1962 he mentioned having read Gibbon through in ten weeks and most of the great historians. In foreign literature he added works of Bossuet, Pascal, Goethe and Schiller. His theological and spiritual reading included Lightfoot's *Apostolic Fathers,* Tertullian's *Apology,* St Augustine's *Homilies on St John's Gospel* and his *de Trinitate,* as well as several volumes of Newman. Given the demands of the monastic horarium this was a remarkable achievement by any standard, and given David's retentive memory it provided a basis for the art of quotation displayed in his historical work. No doubt, too, he was helped by the absence of distraction from a large number of contemporaries, for the lengthening of the war meant that no more novices could be admitted.

When the time for his solemn vows drew near David

was allowed a holiday at home, in July 1918, the first for
four years. No doubt during that time he must have wondered if he was justified in taking solemn vows while the
end of the war was not in sight. Not much news of the
battles would have filtered through to the novitiate, but
every Sunday at the conventual Mass he would have
heard the names read out of those recently fallen. Among
them were at least one in three of his exact school contemporaries. This was a constant reminder of what he had
missed, and in later years he remarked that it was this that
had made him feel the need for a life of greater sacrifice
than that at Downside demanded.

In 1918 Dom Leander Ramsay had been found to be
suffering from an inoperable cancer and he had resigned
as Headmaster. He was given only a few months to live
and returned to the monastery to prepare for the end,
although in the event he was to live for another ten years,
to serve as Abbot for seven of them, and to die of
pneumonia. He now took up again his former studies for
an edition of St Cyprian, and Dom David and Dom Mark
were detailed to assist him for an hour or so each day. This
was a valuable apprenticeship which afforded an opportunity to learn something of the elements of textual criticism under the guidance of an experienced scholar.

With profession behind him David had become a
member of the conventual Chapter and began to be
informed of the problems that affected a large community.
During the war years there had been an absence of
recruits and some deaths of older members, and the Abbot
realised that the growing commitments of the Abbey
would produce a problem of manpower at the end of the
war. There were the needs of Downside itself with its
growing school, the Priory at Ealing, and the large
number of parishes scattered over the whole country, from
Bath to Whitehaven in Cumberland. The parishes were
an inheritance from penal days, indeed from the earliest
history of the revived English Congregation, but by 1918
they had become something of an emotive issue. In the

monastery a generation had grown up that wished to continue in its community life without passing to parochial work, and on monastic principle this outlook was correct. It was a point of view which could be held, while appreciating what other generations had achieved in keeping the faith alive in England, and with thankfulness for the lives of the six members of the community who had died a martyr's death on the scaffold during the seventeenth century. This was the view of Abbot Butler and it became his conviction that parishes would have to be surrendered gradually to the other abbeys or the bishops. It met with natural opposition from those who had spent much of their lives on the parishes, and the solution had to be found by annual votes in conventual Chapter. Of the parishes controlled by Downside in 1918 only three remain today, apart from those served from the Abbey. David followed this problem with great interest and his vote was always given to the motion for surrender.

Among other changes brought about by the end of the war came the reopening of Benet House at Cambridge. In 1896 Christ's College had opened its doors to Downside monks and had thus begun a long and mutually fruitful connection. The day would come when David would be elected an honorary Fellow of the College but in October 1919 he went into residence at Cambridge as an undergraduate with Charles and Mark Pontifex, the former returning to Trinity College. In view of David's academic achievement it may be noted that his examination record in mathematics was inadequate to secure university admission and he was obliged to sit the 'Little-Go' mathematics papers. At Benet House he now found himself living under Dom Bede Camm, a historian of the recusant Catholics and their martyrs. In younger days he had been the author of a romantic work entitled *A Day in the Cloister* and unkind critics were inclined to comment that it was the one day of his life Dom Bede had spent in such precincts. After Westminster School and Keble College, Oxford, Dom Bede had become a Roman Catholic at the same time as an Oxford friend, John Chapman, and both had joined Maredsous Abbey in Belgium. Later they transferred to Downside and served as army chaplains during the war. Dom Bede was kindly, ultra-Tory in outlook and anti-feminist. When an advocate for women's 'lib' wrote to *The Times* demanding equal rights for women at the universities in the name of progress Dom Bede published a reply comparing such progress to that of the Gadarene swine. This did not commend him to the ladies of Girton and Newnham, as he found when chance placed him next to the redoubtable Helen Cam on an archaeological expedition. He was not greatly interested in the young monks who passed through Benet House while he was in charge, but David thought himself fortunate to have had him as Superior at this time.

Christ's had a high standard of classical teaching and the College possessed a formidable trio of classical Fellows in Rackham, Harris Campbell and Sydney Grose. The last of these was senior tutor for many years and a number of Downside undergraduates came under his kindly supervision. He was to provide a model for the tutor, Brown, in C. P. Snow's well-known novel *The Masters*. David was most impressed by Rackham, dry and reserved though he appeared to an undergraduate, for as a teacher he seemed to have a touch of genius. Norman Maclean, an Old Testament and Oriental Languages scholar, and an old friend of Downside's Syriac scholar, Dom Hugh Connolly, was also a college tutor remembered with affection. When I entered Christ's in my turn Maclean had been elected Master, and Grose was my tutor. He is happily still alive in 1979.

The war years spent in the monastery proved no bar to the social life of Cambridge. There was a good contingent of Downside Old Boys in residence, many returned from the Services, and gradually the circle of acquaintance widened as it normally does. A close friendship was formed with one Downside undergraduate, Outram Evennett, who had at this time thoughts of entering the

novitiate. He became a Fellow and tutor of Trinity College
and a historian of the Counter Reformation. At the end of
the first term the three young members of Benet House
were invited to spend two nights at Oxford as the guests of
Francis Urquhart at Balliol. 'Sligger' was an old friend of
Downside and often came over when he stayed with his
uncle at the neighbouring Chewton Priory, then Lord Car-
lingford's home. He met his guests at the station and they
were taken to Balliol by hansom cab, David's first and last
ride of its kind. He admired the social courage of Sligger
when he introduced them to his undergraduates and took
them to dine at high table and lunch in the senior
Common-room. A colleague was inspired to ask if Sligger
was interested in the disposal of college livings. They also
had breakfast in Hall with Downside undergraduates, and
carried away the impression of a relationship at Balliol
between dons and undergraduates which was lacking in
contemporary Cambridge.

Although David had read widely in classical literature
there were gaps in his knowledge, and he had to work hard
to reach the standard of the Tripos. Work was necessary
during the vacation, and during the summer he read the
Iliad and *Odyssey* right through. He never regretted having
studied classics for his degree, regarding this, rightly, as a
sound basis for an historian. In an address to the Anglo-
American Conference of Historians in 1962 he expressed
the view that Roman history 'is a text book without rival
for an historian in training, showing as it does the inexor-
able march of time and the sequence of wisdom and error
and their consequences, in which every problem has been
isolated and debated by some of the acutest minds of
Europe for five centuries.' His undergraduate efforts
brought him great academic success. At the end of his first
year he sat for the inter-collegiate 'Mays' and obtained a
First Class and a college scholarship; in both parts of the
classical Tripos he obtained Firsts, and in the second part
was rewarded with a Distinction in philosophy. This success was not obtained without effort. Having done no

verse he had to start from scratch in his second year so
that he could take the optional papers in Greek and Latin
verse without which First-Class Honours could not be
awarded. The hard grind this involved was typical of the
determination he brought to bear when faced by difficulties. To the university successes he added the Christ's
College Skeat Prize for English literature.

David always considered that the philosophy of Part 2
of the classical Tripos was the most valuable part of his
undergraduate reading, although he found no help from
lecturers. He toiled at Aristotle's *Metaphysics* with the sole
aid of commentaries and found it rewarding. If the University had little to offer in the way of good lecturers on
Aristotle a short course on the *Ethics* was given by Rackham for his pupils, and Cornford was a brilliant lecturer
on the pre-Socratics. David left Cambridge with a lasting
love for Thucydides and claimed that the inspiration for
his first book, on the American Civil War, came, at an
infinite distance, from him. Thucydides appealed to him,
not as perhaps a defective historian, but as the writer
whose characters debate issues which are as real today as
they were in the Athens and Sparta of fourteen hundred
years ago. When David came to teach classics to sixth-
form boys he would tell them that his reading of Plato's
Republic, two or three times, was the most memorable
intellectual experience of his years at Cambridge. In the
last months of his life David became President-elect of the
Classical Association, an honour that gave him great
pleasure coming, as it did, after a life devoted mainly to
historical writing. He mentioned this in a letter to a friend
in 1974:

I somehow feel like Newman when he received the red hat,
that 'the cloud is lifted from me for ever'—the cloud with
which my early classical teachers covered me when they
cursed my stupidity in dealing with North and Hillard and
similar hurdles. . . . There are few gifts of my education that I
value as much as the ability which still remains with me, to

read the *Iliad* or the *Agamemnon* with no more than the occasional failure to know the meaning of a word.

The university period had then been one of intellectual fulfilment and academic success, and there was the added pleasure, when the time came to go down, that his companion at Benet House, Mark Pontifex, had also obtained a First in Classics. In July came ordination to the priesthood at Downside with his former novice master as assistant priest at the first Mass.

A few days at home were spent with his parents during which he visited the house at Baddesley Clinton where the pursuivants had come in 1591 seeking unsuccessfully for the Jesuits hidden within its walls. He remembered the car stopping a little distance from the moat and the almost Elizabethan scene when a maid came from the house and knelt down to kiss his newly consecrated hands. From home he went for one night to visit Stanbrook Abbey, where his cousin, Dame Katharine Loxton, was a nun. Here at evening he looked out of his window in the chaplain's house at the familiar view of the Severn Valley and the slopes of Bredon Hill, and felt envy of the seclusion of this hidden life of the enclosed nuns. So from novitiate to ordination had persisted this awareness of the attraction of a religious life freed from the activities of his own Abbey. Yet if these were his inmost feelings they did not in any way affect his life at Downside.

During these years Dom Aidan Trafford mustered a cricket team in August each year to play teams from the neighbouring villages and occasionally David was a member of the community team. In August 1922 he had a reference to a match in a letter to Outram Evennett: 'On Monday I made no less than 22 runs, Father Thomas and myself putting on about 50 for the 9th wicket! Other performers were . . . his Lordship of Cambysopolis (12 and 19).' His Lordship of Cambysopolis was the assistant Bishop of Westminster, Bishop Butt, who was a regular member of the team for several years.

Shortly after David's ordination Abbot Butler resigned after sixteen years of office and Dom Leander Ramsay was elected in his place, an election that ensured that there would be a continuity of policy. In October David and Mark left for a final year of theological study at the international Benedictine College of Sant' Anselmo in Rome. A month was spent over the journey under the expert guidance of Dom John Chapman, whose knowledge of art and architecture was almost professional and his command of languages wide. This was David's first experience of continental travel and a visit to the Swiss abbey of Einsiedeln, founded in 934, was his first experience of life in an ancient foreign monastery. Italy was entered by the Bernina Pass and days were spent at Venice, Ravenna, Milan, and at Padua in the Abbey which Father Augustine Baker had entered as a novice in the last years of Elizabeth's reign. From there they moved on to Florence, Assisi and Perugia. It was a memorable, if exhausting tour, and on its last section they were held up by the Fascist march on Rome, and David could see history in the making.

Sant' Anselmo, on the Aventine, had not long reopened after the war and the majority of its hundred or so students were German; but there were some Hungarians, Swiss, Italians, Americans, and six Englishmen. At its head was the Abbot Primate, Fidelis von Stotzingen, a former Abbot of Maria Laach in the Rhineland. As a child he had had an English nurse and a French governess and his command of these languages, with Italian, was a great asset. The Abbot Primate's position was not without its difficulties. The office was of no great antiquity and its authority, regarded with suspicion, was merely that of a *primus inter pares*. It was the concern of the national congregations that it should not be used by the Roman Curia as a Trojan horse, to foist centralisation on abbeys that were proud of their autonomy and national characteristics. Fortunately Abbot von Stotzingen was not only a man of culture but also a diplomat. In closer contact with the students was the second-in-command, an American, and the English students were under the charge of a Belgian, Dom Lambert Beaudoin, who, having a great affection for England, allowed them freedom to take full advantage of the cultural opportunities afforded by a stay in Rome.

For an Englishman, life at Sant' Anselmo was not easy; there was no heating in winter and the food was austere, yet David found the régime of the college less physically demanding than life at Downside. He was not greatly impressed by the theological teaching, the Latin lectures with an absence of tutorials and the *viva* examinations also in Latin. But he was not following the major course and so had no contact with four lecturers whose reputation impressed him as that of men who would have been welcomed in any university: the Hungarian Justinian Seredi, authority on canon law, the metaphysician Joseph Gredt, Hildebrand Höpfl, a distinguished biblical scholar, and Philibert Schmitz, who was later to edit the *Revue Bénédictine*. In 1935 when Justinian Seredi was a cardinal and Prince Primate of Hungary he came to Downside as papal legate to consecrate the Abbey church. On that occasion it is recorded that his flowing colloquial Latin surprised and impressed the Dean and Chapter of Gloucester when they gave him a formal reception.

There were now opportunities to explore Rome, and the Campagna, and early-morning walks to celebrate Mass in that loveliest of churches, Santa Maria in Cosmedin, followed by a cup of coffee in its sacristy. At Easter, visits were made to Monte Cassino and Subiaco, with a brief stay at Naples guided by Dom Urban Butler. Dom Urban was then attending on Cardinal Gasquet at the Palace of San Callisto in Rome but the Cardinal himself showed no interest in his young brethren from Downside. Occasionally friends from England came to Sant' Anselmo, and Sligger Urquhart brought a trio of undergraduates from Oxford: Roger Mynors, Bobbie Longden and Cyril Connolly. There was also tea at the British School with its eminent Director, Eugenia Strong.

At the end of the academic year David and Dom Mark took their *viva* examinations in Latin before a panel of lecturers and left for the Abbey of Monte Vergine near Naples, staying first in the winter house of the community and then climbing four thousand feet through oak and beech woods to the main Abbey. The journey was made on mule back. Monte Vergine had had a continuous existence since its foundation in about 1100 by St William, and at this time there still clung about it something of the atmosphere described by the Prince of Lampedusa in his *Leopard*. David gave an account of the site in a letter home:

> wedged between the rocks a few hundred feet short of the summit, among woods of beech and hazel, and turf covered with every kind of wild flower. Below, the rocks fall in precipices so that from the windows you look down on the tops of trees and village roofs thousands of feet below. In the woods all round the house are the cows, and the sound of their bells supplies the music of our mountain torrents at home. From the pass above is a view over the bays of Naples and Salerno on one side—with Vesuvius smoking away and Capri behind in the haze—and the provinces of Benevento and Apulia and the Basilicata on the other. The mountains are very desert, and there are wolves in plenty, keeping themselves to themselves this summer weather, but in winter possessing the hills and coming down to howl round the monastery.
>
> Everything about the place seems fated to be unique. There is an old rule, dating from St William, that no meat, milk, eggs or cheese be eaten in the house—an impossible rule in these latter days, so a second refectory has been built where such things can be eaten at certain meals, and, there being no room for it in this cleft of rock, it has been set in another, approached by a tunnel cut out in the living rock, or in these days of summer, by a path along the face of the rock with the most superb views over the plain and mountains beyond to the Adriatic.

A leisurely return to England was made by way of Salerno, La Cava Abbey, Pisa, Siena and so home. In later years David's judgements of individuals and communities tended to be rigorous and exacting, and it is interesting to note his verdict on Sant' Anselmo, written to Abbot Ramsay before leaving:

> ... The better one gets to know the people here, officials and students, the more one is struck by the immense goodness and charity of them all—without any affectation or exaggeration—it is really most edifying. I cannot help thinking sometimes that if such are the results of training in modern Benedictine houses then Benedictines as a whole have nothing to be ashamed of. Downside seems to be well known and admired ... somehow they all seem to have received the idea that the community is very learned—as indeed it is, but not quite in the way they conceive.

Chapter Four

AT WORK IN THE COMMUNITY

Today has been the loveliest of the year—the fresh green
of the beeches and elms—that unbelievable green that
grows darker almost as you watch it, that makes you
catch your breath and almost feel pain at such beauty.

Verweile doch, du bist so schön

Tulips and crab blossom and cherries all under the
beeches and sycamore in front of the monastery—and in
it that passage of youth—all the opening of eyes and
hearts—that Downside gives.

D. K. to A. M., 1929

David returned to Downside at the end of 1923 to live
under a much admired new Abbot. In the previous January he had written from Rome to Abbot Ramsay on the
occasion of his solemn Blessing:

I do so wish I could be at Downside for it. . . . To those of us
who were in the school when you were Head the day is even
more memorable than it is for others, I think, because you are
inseparably linked in our memories with the Downside we
first learnt to love . . . and in such memories of Downside
you will always have a part.

It was the opening of a new chapter not only for David but
also for the community, with the novitiate, empty for most

47

of the war, beginning to fill again and a sense of new life felt by all.

In October of this year I entered the novitiate with five others and, considering that the novices met the community only once a week for a bare half-hour on Sundays, I was soon on fairly intimate terms with Father David. This was understandable. At this stage it seemed to a new novice that the middle section of the community was absorbed in its work and interests while David and Dom Mark were not yet caught up in great activity. They, too, suffered from a lack of contemporaries and were therefore more approachable. Emerging as one did once a week from the confinement and unintellectual life of the novitiate David's personality made a deep impression and he was a most stimulating companion. The discipline of the novitiate tended to make its members feel that they were back again in the fourth form at school. Most novices took some months to adapt to the demands of a strange life and to lose the awkwardness involved in performing unfamiliar duties under the critical eyes of the community. David had the gift of communicating his own cheerfulness, his wide interests, and seeming self-confidence. He had passed through the ugly-duckling stage himself and remembered being rebuked by Edmund Bishop for some awkwardness shown in a liturgical function. By the end of my novitiate year we were firm friends. For the next six years, until I was sent abroad for theological studies, I served his Mass every morning after the choir Office. It became an annual custom for us to walk to Wells during the Christmas season, climbing over Penn Hill and attending Evensong in the Cathedral. Penn Hill today is disfigured by a tall television mast but for me it still retains something of the magic of that time when 'to be young was very heaven'.

David's self-confidence was perhaps more apparent than real. In fact he felt diffident and apprehensive at the thought of teaching in the school. A year earlier the Headmaster had asked that he should undertake some

sixth-form teaching but the Abbot had refused, unwilling
to deprive him of the year in Rome. I was myself much
later thrown into sixth-form teaching and the work of a
Housemaster as soon as my studies were completed. Surprisingly in David's case his first year's work was to consist of coaching a single boy for a university scholarship
and a junior scripture class. The boy was an exceptional
one and at the end of the year he secured a major award at
Trinity College, Cambridge, and distinctions in Greek,
Latin, and Ancient History in the Higher Certificate
examination. A whole year teaching one boy, however
able, was not without difficulty and tedium, but out of it
was forged a friendship which lasted until David's death.

This first year at Downside as a priest was full of interest in other ways. Few religious communities of that time
can have possessed such varied abilities among its members, such strong personalities, and in daily life such live-
liness and wit. I remember the impression made by the
brilliant conversation and ready repartee of the senior
Fathers, ranging over wide fields, which I received when
finally released into the community from the novitiate.
The irreverent title of the 'Athenaeum' was given by the
young to one such group. At the community gathering
after dinner one might pass from a group, possibly including Dean Armitage Robinson of Wells, which was arguing
the correct translation of a line of a medieval Latin poem,
by way of one discussing the Test Match to a description
of an encounter with the inhabitants of Afghanistan. Ten
years later David found his community still impressive for
these and deeper qualities. There was the group of elderly
scholars who set the tone: Abbot Ramsay, his new Prior,
Dom John Chapman, Dom Hugh Connolly, and the well-
known Somerset archaeologist, Dom Ethelbert Horne,
who was parish priest of the village which he ruled with
almost autocratic sway, having baptised the majority of its
inhabitants and blessed their weddings. It was believed by
some of us, on no firm ground, that the villagers voted
Liberal *en masse* at parliamentary elections in deference to

Dom Ethelbert's well-known political opinions. Among those younger in age were two who had an important role to play later at a critical point of David's life: the remarkable Headmaster, Dom Sigebert Trafford, and the Bursar, Dom Bruno Hicks, a man of charm and culture if not a strong personality. From time to time distinguished visitors came to share the life of the community and a special friend was the neighbouring Dean of Wells, Armitage Robinson, who tried to guide David into the field of patristic study. The Dean's encouragement was readily given to young students, and I remember discussions with him on medieval topics in the Deanery of Wells, with a break after lunch for his inevitable siesta. The scholarly Bishop Burton of Clifton was another welcome visitor, and younger members of the community found amusement in his erudite confirmation addresses to the prep-school boys with their occasional references to Tertullian.

Yet if there was happiness and fulfilment, tensions were not wholly absent. No member of a monastic community involved in the work of a large school and with pastoral responsibility for its local villages can escape an occasional awareness of the contradiction between its activity and the enclosed, secluded life envisaged in the Rule of St Benedict. David possibly felt this more than most and perhaps the more so because he so much enjoyed the new activities that came his way. He had not lost his early attraction to a stricter form of monastic life and on this problem he was greatly helped both by the example and the understanding of Abbot Ramsay.

During the summer David undertook to supply the Sunday duties, in the absence on holiday of the parish priest, at Midsomer Norton, one of the local parishes served from the Abbey. In preparation he learned to drive a car and was more successful than a contemporary who was abnormally unmechanical. The latter had managed to drive a small car up the terraces in front of the monastery and had remained there, alarmed and disconsolate, until another monk had arrived to manoeuvre it down.

This was David's first experience of pastoral work and he found it rewarding. The church was a large and attractive medieval barn which had been well adapted for its purpose, and the congregation, mostly converts, included a large group of young men who took an active part in the services. He was conscious of an atmosphere of devotion and enthusiasm and continued to supply there for four summers.

At the end of term David accepted an invitation from Sligger Urquhart to spend a fortnight in his chalet in the Haute Savoie. As Dean of Balliol Sligger was an Oxford institution and his Chalet des Mélèzes, high in the Alps above St Gervais, was his summer home where since the 1890s he had welcomed a series of Oxford undergraduates during the long vacations. Urquhart had a flair for selecting guests of future distinction. David had already met Roger Mynors, Bobbie Longden and Cyril Connolly in Rome, and now he met for the first time Tom Boase, historian and future President of Magdalen College, and Kenneth Clark the distinguished art historian and critic. Some, including Cyril Connolly, were to pay visits in the future to Downside. Stories tended to accumulate around the chalet parties, and Cyril Bailey, in his memoir of Sligger, related how the Abbé Klein, observing three members of the party, all sons of bishops, setting off for a walk was heard to murmur: '*Trois fils d'evêques; tiens c'est drôle.*' David remembered an occasion when Cyril Connolly and others had suddenly decided to bathe in a mountain pool. As Cyril Connolly entered the water a clear female voice was heard from the midst of some neighbouring bushes: '*Mon Dieu! Encore un homme nu.*' David was a guest at the chalet on four occasions and the young men he met there included the present Lord Hailsham, John Sparrow of All Souls, Douglas Jay, Roy Harrod and William Hayter.

The new school year opened with a heavier load of work and he found himself in charge of the classical upper sixth, coming into contact with a group of able boys whose confidence was soon won. Respect and affection developed on both sides and David found himself enjoying something of a honeymoon period. His working day was now a very full one, probably excessively so. He attended all the church services save for the conventual Mass and began teaching in the mornings at 9.30. Afternoons were spent supervising junior games with more teaching in the evenings, but there was time for a second half-hour of mental prayer before Vespers, and time for private reading after the 8.30 pm Compline. Yet this was brief, and seven hours of sleep could be secured only by lights out at 10 pm, for morning Mattins began at 5.20. There were occasional free afternoons when he could walk or cycle, but he had volunteered to take a junior game although he grudged the long summer hours devoted to cricket with a group of unskilful junior boys. Our modern practice of releasing the unwilling and incompetent from organised games did not obtain in that day. David found all this frustrating, but I remember as a novice passing him on my way to manual labour as he came down from the cricket field with a group of young boys. It was a happy group, relaxed and bubbling with talk, and one I never forgot. It confirmed all the impressions of David that I had gleaned from the brief Sunday meetings in the monastic calefactory. This heavy programme was to continue for some time, and in 1927 he referred to his activities in a letter to Outram Evennett: 'I have really been most terribly busy this last fortnight. In addition to classics I run a sodality, lectures, and an under-15 rugger side.' David had once commented in a letter to Abbot Ramsay from Rome that life at Downside was 'physically very, very exacting, if not excessively so', and in after-life he wondered at the amount of work accomplished in a single week at this time. Yet amidst all this activity he found time for writing during school holidays. In 1926 a short book appeared on the American Civil War and in the following year a short study of the English mystics.

In December 1926 two of David's pupils won open awards at Cambridge, at Trinity and Clare, and he took them up to the university Greek play, the *Electra* of Sophocles, in which a former pupil, Jack Hamson, had a part. This visit inspired plans for a walking tour with them in Greece during the summer holidays and David wrote an account of their odyssey for the *Downside Review*. Significantly in later years he thought of this holiday as a betrayal of his monastic convictions. Judged by the number of university awards obtained by his pupils, the years of teaching, if brief, were very successful and several of his pupils later achieved distinction in their careers. His first pupil, Jack Hamson, held a Fellowship of Trinity College and a Cambridge Chair of Law; Helenus Milmo became a judge and was brought in by the Foreign Office to investigate the Burgess, Maclean and Philby scandal. Joe Maloney became an eminent Queen's Counsel, a legal knight, and Chairman of the General Council of the Bar, while David Drummond, later Earl of Perth, served as a Minister of the Crown. Denys Hamson died young, after service with the partisans in Greece and in France during the war.

For David these years of teaching brought an increase of maturity and confidence. He was always conscious of a lonely childhood and in spite of a happy family background seems always to have been reaching out for affection, uncertain if it would be given. In 1930 he expressed something of this in a letter to me: 'I can never really trust friendship, partly because I am so selfish in my affections, I suppose, partly because (as I suppose we all do) I always think myself less changeable than other people. What complicated creatures we are.' It may be that he never recovered completely from the rebuff he had experienced in his schooldays from the one boy whose close friendship he most desired. Now he had gained in self-confidence from the knowledge that he could control and direct boys in class and games, and still more that he could win their affection. However, the activity and interests of these years were not allowed to affect his spiritual life. Each year he re-read works of St Teresa, St John of the Cross and

Father Baker, and the Carthusian life was still dimly seen as a way of escape from what at times appeared to be a Downside compromise between the spirit and the world.

As Abbot, Dom Leander Ramsay tended to be secretive about his plans and it was from a casual conversation with the Headmaster that David learned at Easter that he was to be sent to Cambridge, to replace Dom Bede Camm at Benet House. This came as a complete surprise, and the summer term of 1928 was therefore destined to bring to an end his teaching career in the school. It was suddenly cut short by a driving accident. Early in July David was driven to Midsomer Norton for the Sunday service and at a cross-road the small car was in collision with a lorry. David was flung through the windscreen and suffered serious concussion, a cracked cheekbone and a deep cut across the temple. The school doctor was fetched from Downside and David was removed to the hospital at Paulton where it was feared that he might lose the sight of one eye. When recovery was under way a haemorrhage occurred late one night and the staff were unable for some time to arrest the bleeding. After a month in the hospital he was moved to the infirmary at Downside and during his convalescence was told by the Abbot that he was to spend the next year as temporary Novice Master. The health of the official Novice Master had caused some anxiety and he was to spend a year in South Africa as guest of the parents of one of the younger monks. There were those later who believed that the accident had left a permanent mark and had changed David's character. While he believed that his experience had given him freedom of spirit, others traced to it an obstinacy and inflexibility that developed after that time. Certain it is that from this time on he sometimes revealed a harshness of judgement unknown before, and not for him was the maxim of St Augustine: *Flectamur facile ne frangamur*—'Let us bend easily, lest we be broken.'

It was no easy matter for David to part from contact with the school. He always thought that during the short period of his teaching some of the most gifted and attractive boys to be found anywhere had passed through Downside. It was an effort to accept the loss of contact with such lively and enquiring minds and he returned to this four years later in a letter to me:

> I would never have believed that I could bear to leave the school—I could never have left it of myself, I am so weak— you have no idea how I loved it. It was done for me and·I am far happier. God never fails to bless the least sacrifice, even if it is merely making a virtue out of necessity.

Nevertheless the weeks he spent preparing for the introductory Retreat for the new novices were a time of peace, for he was determined to give himself wholly to God's guidance. Moreover, for the first time he now had a position of responsibility to the community and he would still be in contact with young minds. He had never been unhappy since he first entered the monastery and now he adjusted to a new rhythm of his life. He moved to the large cell on the top floor of the monastery which the Novice Master traditionally occupied, with its wide views across the Mendips and across lawns and trees to the cricket field. In September he welcomed seven new postulants, of whom five were to survive the course. The new entrants, of whom five came from the school, were in their different ways a gifted group, and of the eleven who were professed during the next two years five held first-class university degrees of Oxford and Cambridge.

David was also in charge of the young monks in simple vows who by custom remained under the Novice Master's care for two years after simple profession. He also had the task of teaching dogmatic theology to a group of Juniors in the community. A Novice Master has a heavy responsibility. It is on his judgement, based on close observation, that a religious community must rely when it is called upon to vote on candidates for profession, and this was especially so at a time when the novices were much more separated from the community than they are today. In the main, David looked for a capacity for love and a nature receptive of truth, guided by the chapter of advice provided by St Benedict in his Rule. There he tells the Novice Master that he must try his best to see if the novice is truly seeking God, if he is eager for the work of God [the choral Office], for obedience, and for humiliations. The novice must be clearly warned of the hardships and difficulties of the life he is seeking. David lacked experience for this difficult office and always thought he had held too light a rein, with too little of the *dura et aspera,* but his capacity to evoke affection had not deserted him. Those who came under his care at this time, without exception, looked back with affection and admiration for his guidance.

At this point it is necessary to turn to events in the life of the community in so far as they affected David's outlook. For six years he had been living under the rule of an Abbot for whom he had whole-hearted respect, shared by a younger generation who had been growing up in the monastery responsive to the distinction of mind and character of Abbot Ramsay, and very conscious of the Abbot's personal care for them. This deep affection for the Abbot did not always imply or call for entire agreement with all his policies, and there was awareness of problems which called for solution. Abbot Ramsay had always supported the policies of his predecessor and was determined that his young monks should be able to look forward to permanent residence in the monastery. He continued the policy of surrendering parishes, but more difficult for some was the question of future policy in regard to the school. During the ten years that Dom Sigebert Trafford had been Headmaster the reputation of the school, already high, had grown. Intellectual standards had been maintained, but in this department the Headmaster himself had little to contribute. He was, however, fortunate to have had the services of some first-class teachers from the community and he had a flair for selecting good laymasters. His own special achievement had been to increase the reputation of Downside in the major school games. Downside had

become a leading rugger school, and the present Earl of
Lytton has recorded his impressions of Dom Sigebert's
influence in this field.[1] In the early 1920s three of his Old
Boys had played in the university match while another
was Captain of Hockey at Cambridge, to be followed by
Maurice Turnbull as Captain of Cricket and later as Captain of Glamorgan. Meanwhile other members of the
Turnbull family had been winning rugger caps for Wales.
There was no doubt about Dom Sigebert's powers of leadership, of his ease and charm, or of his control of discipline. Yet to Dom David and others there were less pleas-
ing aspects of his régime.

The Headmaster seemed to lack a real appreciation of
academic ability or regard boys of unusual ability as valuable members of the school in their own right. He was also
unable to share or delegate responsibility. The exigencies
of wartime had left him in sole control and when it ended
he admitted no colleague to share responsibility. His exact
contemporary, Dom Austin Corney, a man of similar
unintellectual tastes but gifted with great understanding
of young boys, was in charge of the preparatory section, a
post he held under the Headmaster for nearly seventeen
years. Younger members of the community had to accept
their exclusion from any position of delegated authority
such as Dom Anselm Rutherford gave his Housemasters
in my day. In the winter of 1927–8 David asked for an
interview with the Headmaster and expressed his views on
the absence of intellectual influence and of delegation. He
was given a friendly hearing, but Dom Sigebert made it
clear that he could not conduct the school in any other
way.

At this point David, as a member of the teaching staff,
was interested and concerned about the need for a
stronger spiritual and intellectual influence. He was not in
any way critical of the work of the school as suitable for a
monastic community. A few months later when he had

[1] See *The Desert and the Green*

ceased to be a member of the teaching staff his attitude
began to change, a result no doubt of increasing interest in
the contemplative life and the teaching of St John of the
Cross. In time he came to regard the development of the
school as a menace to the spiritual life of the community,
and as likely to nullify the movement for reform of which
Abbot Cuthbert Butler had been a leading figure. A hint
of this can be read in his memoir of the Abbot, published
in 1934. He never changed this opinion. More than thirty
years later he wrote in *Christian Monasticism* (p. 242): 'It is
difficult to see how the running of a large school ... can
be reconciled in the modern world with the monastic vocation.' It must be emphasised that during all this period no
member of the community was permitted to teach in the
school or undertake any activity connected with it until his
theological studies had been completed. It was not permitted to enter the school buildings during term or to watch a
school match. The lives of the novices and junior monks
proceeded as though no school existed, apart from the
presence of boys in the Abbey church or the distant sound
of school bells. This régime covered nearly thirty of us.

It was, however, in another field that David found himself involved in current problems. Abbot Ramsay had
great designs for the future of the Abbey and was immediately concerned with the need for more accommodation
for a growing community and for a permanent library
building. In 1928 he was able to offer plans for approval
by the Chapter. The nave of the Abbey church had not
long been completed by Sir Giles Scott, but for domestic
buildings the Abbot turned to the architect of Bristol University, Sir George Oatley. The plans were approved by a
large majority at the conventual Chapter but then the
Abbot had second thoughts and a new, enlarged and more
costly scheme was put forward.

Had this scheme gone ahead the result might have been
of significance for David's future as it is unlikely that a
foundation could have been made at Worth in 1933. A
majority of the Council approved the new plan but opposi-

tion persisted and was led by the Prior and Headmaster. I
was now at Cambridge and would have known little of the
matter, but David corresponded and kept me informed. In
January 1929 he wrote:

> The political situation is still very tense. . . . It has always
> been painful to differ from the Abbot—I hate the feeling of
> differing from an abbot, simply because he is abbot *et vices
> Christi creditur agere in monasterio*, and our Abbot has always
> been to me a model and exemplar of religious virtue. . . .
> Don't think I am depressed—it is in a way deeper than
> depression—it is the horrible feeling of having to judge one
> whom I hoped to be able always to love and reverence *simplic-
> iter* and without reserve.

At first the Abbot refused to consider any alternative to his
plans but two weeks later David wrote again:

> Lest I be thought to terrify you with my epistles I hasten to
> let you know that the tension is somewhat relaxed. A Council
> was held on Tuesday and at the last moment the Abbot told
> Sigebert that he would agree to the free and full discussion of
> any alternative plan, save one on the East, if the four council-
> lors withdrew their letter [of opposition]. After that there was
> going and coming and I received visits from not a few of the
> Fathers who were trying to square their minds to swallow a
> formula (if you see what I mean). I felt—*si parva licet componere
> magnis*—not unlike an impartial witness of the scene at Lam-
> beth described by Sir Thomas More. . . . However, ultimately
> a formula—of almost super anglican vagueness, a perfect
> cloud of verbiage, was produced. At a chapter in April two
> plans are to be brought up 1) the Abbot's January plan 2) an
> alternative. . . .

At this point the Abbot fell ill with influenza which
developed into pneumonia, and after a brief illness he
died. To his community the loss of a well-loved Superior
was tragic and to none more than to David. No doubt his
thoughts went back to his boyhood when Dom Leander
was the first Downside monk he had met, and to the years

that had followed as a boy in the school under an admired and respected Headmaster. Sixty years after their first meeting he commented on Leander Ramsay in a letter to Abbot Trafford: 'After a lifetime in which I have come across many of the most distinguished minds at Cambridge, Oxford and other universities, I still think that he had qualities which I have never met elsewhere.' David also once remarked that, as Abbot, Dom Leander had drawn Sparta in the lottery of his later years. Elected to the abbacy near the age of sixty he had felt the need to move slowly in order to carry with him those who did not altogether agree with his policies. Had he lived he would certainly have been re-elected for a second term of office and would have had the devoted support of a large number of monks professed during his abbacy. Hitherto David's life had been moving forward smoothly. His gifts of mind and character had begun to single him out and there were already some who looked to him for future leadership. With the death of Abbot Ramsay clouds began to gather.

Chapter Five

A CHANGE OF DIRECTION

I would admit that I have changed since 1926.
                                    D. K. to A. M., 1931

During the interregnum of a month before the abbatial
election could be held authority rested with the Prior. He
was Dom John Chapman, whose name has been mentioned earlier and whom Abbot Ramsay had recalled in
1923 from his work at Rome as a member of the Vulgate
Commission. No doubt Ramsay appreciated his distinction as a scholar but it was a curious appointment, for
Dom John was not at all well known to the community,
having transferred from the Beuron Congregation in 1913
with absence from Downside as an army chaplain for
much of the war. He was first and foremost a deeply
spiritual monk whose *Spiritual Letters,* published after his
death, have had an enduring influence. He was also a man
of unusual temperament, interesting, unpredictable,
amusing but never quite able to follow the community
humour at Downside, which sometimes puzzled him.
David always thought of him as the possessor of the most
brilliant and versatile mind that he had ever known but
they were never really in sympathy. As Prior Dom John
also held the office of Junior Master and was well liked by
his young men, of whom I was one, but to some senior
members he did not appear to be a 'typical' Downside
monk.

Few members of the community had thought of him as a likely candidate for the abbacy. Seniors were a little suspicious of his early training in a foreign monastery, and younger men, while they regarded him with affectionate amusement, considered him to be much too volatile and indiscreet. Abbot Ramsay's death, however, had left something of a vacuum; while as acting Superior the Prior impressed us as being both fatherly and sensible. When the day of the election arrived most of the younger members of the conventual Chapter voted for him, while others gave him their votes as for an elderly candidate who would not have more than one term of office, a sort of Pope John XXIII. Once elected, Dom John soon resumed his former *persona* and the indecision which delayed his appointment of a Prior was typical. No other changes of officials were made: Dom Sigebert Trafford had now been Headmaster for eleven years and Dom Bruno Hicks Bursar for fourteen. Like many scholars who are not themselves businesslike Abbot Chapman had an admiration for practical men and he had great respect for Dom Sigebert as an administrator of decision. He had, as Prior, indicated to me and to others his opinion that a change of officials was overdue and, as it became clear that the *status quo* was to be maintained, a certain disillusionment with the new régime began to surface. Abbot Ramsay had in some respects been unyielding but had respected the right of others to hold their own opinions; the new Abbot seemed to be more autocratic and intolerant of criticism.

The Ramsay building plans were now put aside, and the immediate problem of accommodation for a growing community was relieved by the erection of a temporary wing above the East Cloister. In May 1929 David wrote to me at Cambridge:

Not a hint yet of any building activities, and except that the Abbot, like man's free will, is always capable of changing against all probability, I should say there will be none. The money will go elsewhere and in four or five years the 'White

House' will be as full as the present monastery. It seems a sad
end to a whole series of events ... spiritually and intellectually a new monastery and library would be of untold value.

David's forecast proved correct and Downside had to
wait until after the Second World War for a new and
permanent monastery wing and library. A steady series of
new school buildings took precedence, beginning with a
science wing. Amid much that gave cause for disappointment, younger members of the community secured the
election of David to the Abbot's Council, half of its members being elected annually by the *conventus* and the rest
nominated by the Abbot. This was a measure of the
respect and affection David had won.

By now, and it was significant, he was tending to the
view that holidays were not justified in the monastic life
but part of August was spent touring with his father and
for the fourth and last time he joined the party at
Urquhart's chalet, with Dom Charles Pontifex, Roger
Mynors, Humphrey Sumner and Tom Boase. On his way
home he spent two days at Solesmes, as a guest of Dom
Noetinger, the translator of the English mystics, and he
sent a brief account of this visit to Outram Evennett: 'The
brethren were extremely kind and sociable and the chant
quite *inoubliable*. They sang so perfectly that at the end of
each familiar antiphon I longed for an encore—rhythm
and all the choir exactly together. I attended a lecture by
the choirmaster.'

These impressions contrast with those of a visit to
another abbey:

I did not strike anyone whom I wanted to meet again very
much although they are most monastic and edifying. There
are several strata in the community: the oldy, mouldy, hoary
Tory aristocratic element and [others] of every degree of
intelligence and refinement. There is plenty of life but no
charm or distinction, at least I found none. But the place
clearly has a future of good religious life and work before it.

David now waited to hear from the Abbot about his own future work. He would have liked to continue as Novice Master, but the official Novice Master had returned as part of a conservative administration. He did not think, and rightly as it proved, that the Abbot would remove his old friend, Dom Bede Camm, from Benet House, but he asked to be kept out of the school. In the event he was appointed Junior Master, in charge of all the young monks who were not priests and who were not in the novitiate. It was an office that I held briefly later under Abbot Trafford. He also continued to teach theology and became editor of the *Downside Review*, a quarterly now in its fiftieth year that had fallen away from its once high standard. During David's editorship it was to reach distinction again and to publish a number of his early articles on monastic history.

The year 1930 marked a change of direction which had influenced his request to be excluded from work in the school. A letter of rebuke sent to me at Cambridge some months earlier had foreshadowed a new austerity:

> You will soon be too old to listen to the voice of one giving advice, charm he never so wisely, and you mustn't resent my *fervor novitiorum magister*. In brief, I was more than half serious in my disapproval of your wanderings. I didn't like your visit to the *Dream of Gerontius,* nor really your so-long sojourn at Oxford. It is terribly easy to accept every attractive invitation, to make new friends, to have new and delightful experiences—and then to feel that one must get away from Downside again and again during the year. You will say— what business of mine what you do? None, if I were trying to speak merely as a setter right of my brother, prosecuting a search for motes. But if I speak out of affection, because it does make a great difference to me what you do, perhaps you will allow the right. I feel that we agree upon so many things and you are the only one below me (in conventual order not in merit!) who reasons with life in most aspects much as I do. Consequently I look to you more than to most to be in time a sign to an unbelieving generation, a people that hath stiff

necks. (This sounds very self-righteous but is not meant so very seriously.) But it's useless to preach principles one doesn't practise.... If a stay-at-home, choir-frequenting not-worldly monk is to be our ideal, we must act the part ourselves. All the rest must go.... You may say my own example is bad. So it is at times. My visit to Cambridge for the Greek play was probably unjustifiable—and possibly the Greek tour.... You have no idea what a stabilising influence the Abbot [Ramsay] was when Headmaster by refusing to go here, there and everywhere when invited.

Don't think me too puritanical. Star differeth from star, and there must be some latitude at Downside.... I cease being novice master tomorrow and therefore can afford to be less pompous. I am facing the Tudors again and reading the Stonor, Cely and Plumpton letters. Once more, you mustn't mind my offering you a word of godly counsel.

Gradually David began to drop many outside interests, to give up playing tennis or squash, the reading of fiction and listening to music. Television did not exist and radio was not permitted in the monastery. His life became more secluded and free of external distraction. Increasingly he attempted to follow the ascetical teaching of St John of the Cross above all other spiritual writers, and as part of the general renunciation he decided to pay no more visits to Urquhart's chalet. In 1931 he spent a few days at Quarr Abbey in the Isle of Wight, where he had the opportunity to observe Benedictine life in a contemplative monastery belonging to the Congregation of France. During this visit he found in the library the two volumes of Garrigou-Lagrange's *Perfection Chrétienne et Contemplation* and his reading of this work made a profound impression. From its author he learnt that the first commandment was an absolute one which might not be realised in its fullness all at once but must be observed to the height of one's powers here and now, and more fully in the light of God's future gift. He saw this as a contrast to the doctrine that distinguished between commands and counsels, as a contrast to the idea that, although the vows of religion carried an obligation to tend towards perfection, sanctity was not for the ordinary man. The visit to Quarr was followed by one to the Cistercian Abbey of Mount St Bernard in Leicester-shire.

In the autumn of 1931 David was asked to substitute for the Abbot and give the annual Retreat for the Good Shepherd nuns in London. He was deeply impressed by this community and wrote to a friend:

> They are marvellous people. I have never before been right up against high spirituality (and by that I mean, literally, the heights, seen not in the realm of books, but in simple, hardly literate lay sisters, who are led simply by God himself, and without having read about it, to the ultimate stages described by St Teresa and St John of the Cross). One learns in the way of experience more by coming across a few such than by any amount of reading. The Mother Provincial, who is saintly herself, is perfectly common sense and is an excellent guide to them all. The work they do is extraordinary, too, taking girls off the streets.

To him the life of this community seemed to signify exactly what was meant by abandonment of all that was not the love of God. He was both impressed and humbled by such fervour, and the experience of this Retreat confirmed him in the path on which he was now moving.

Meanwhile at home David was becoming conscious of an increasing lack of sympathy between him and the Abbot, and at meetings of the Council their views seldom agreed. A clash occurred over the profession of a Junior. It was the custom for the Junior Master to state his views and report to both the Council and the conventual Chapter: David opposed this profession, the Abbot was strongly in favour. He mentioned the affair in a letter to me:

> I am in deep waters (*sub sigillo* this).... The Abbot will see no arguments or even good intentions in me on this subject—which is saddening.

Allein und abgetrennt
von aller Freude

How hard it is to keep people's sympathy unless you tell them
what they want to hear. All this has gone towards teaching
me a lesson—I may be wrong and too may refuse to understand people. For heaven's sake never say anything to me on
any subject that you don't really feel—and if you ever think
that I do not judge right say so. One may as well have a few
friends one can be frank with, for really I have been saddened
by too many differences of opinion in the past years.

At this time I was studying theology at the university in
Munich. When I returned to Downside for the university
vacation I had occasion to take him at his word. Hitherto
many of us had looked to him for leadership, in agreement
with his vision for the future of our community and
inspired by his religious example. On my return from
Germany I began to sense something which caused me
uneasiness. David had adopted practices, small in themselves and of no great importance, which were not common to the community as a whole. Now I found that some
of his Juniors had begun to copy these externals, members
of a small group on whom a contemporary had bestowed
the name of the 'Spirituals'. I felt that here was a possible
source of division and criticism which David should bring
to an end. It was no easy matter to raise this with someone
who was both senior and the subject of great regard and I
failed to make my object clear; there was some misunderstanding. However, when I returned abroad I received a
revealing letter:

... I would admit that I have changed since 1926—we all
have, but my change, *tel quel,* has not been a volte-face, but
rather trying to practise what I would always have preached.
This you should have realised, I think even if you did not
approve. And you should have realised too, shouldn't you,
that my indiscretion or stupidity in regard to you was not the
result of disapproval but of affection. I can't ever drift away

from people. If they have been a great part of my life they
remain so, long after they have forgotten me ... I do not
think myself to have attained but I am sure that what I am
preaching is true—is in fact a truism. It is that the way of
renunciation, of the Cross, is the only one—and that the
renunciation must be of ourselves—affections, hopes,
activities. . . . Do you again say here that 1926 was better. I
know it is not so. I *know* that I have a peace now which I had
not then.

During the year 1932 the conventual Chapter was called to decide upon a matter of unusual importance: the
purchase of Milton Abbey in Dorset. It was a property of
special appeal to a monastic community, of great natural
beauty at this time before the surrounding woods had
been felled, but most of all on account of the pre-
Reformation Abbey church and a wing of the monastic
buildings which were intact and in perfect repair. Abbot
Chapman was enthusiastic when first approached by its
owners and he decided that if the support of the Chapter
could be won he would place a community at Milton and
move the preparatory school there from Downside, with
the hope that within a few years the foundation would
become autonomous. He also hoped to use the foundation
as a reason for surrendering more of our parishes. David
gave his full support to this project:

I am and have been for several weeks entirely and
confirmedly for Milton—that is I think it is in every way our
duty to take it—more, that I feel it has been given us almost
visibly as God's providence. . . . You will have heard of the
Abbot's *peregrinatio ad limina.* Yesterday we received an epistle
from without the Flaminian Gate and today I believe he is to
return. To judge by the letter, he got an unequivocal statement from the Holy Father that religious should not live on
parishes; that is good, excellent in fact. . . . I expect that Milton will be voted *nem.con.* and I expect only 15 or so against
the relinquishing of parishes.

This letter, sent to one of his Juniors studying theology abroad, not only showed his support for the new foundation but included a statement of great importance when we come to consider his own future:

> Remember then, always even at the darkest, that you must aim at the highest—*perfectus esto*—and it will be only your fault (because God always helps) if you don't attain. Never blame it on Downside. The contemplative life—contemplative prayer—is possible even at Downside.

I was unable to attend the Chapter but David sent me an account:

> ... Psychologically I think the note is of great satisfaction at work done combined with singularly little of that crusading feeling and a deeper feeling that the future is really the test. ... Altogether one felt that the occasion was historic, rather because of the votes registered than because of the ideas or ideals expressed or even felt. The Abbot's conduct of the business was really quite (if not very) good. He somehow never inspires like Butler or Ramsay did, but he got things done this time better than them. Now we can really say that the future lies wih us and that we can really lead the Congregation once again. It will only be our fault if we fail.

During the negotiations for the purchase of Milton a difficulty had emerged which at first had seemed unimportant. An eighteenth-century owner had removed the village to a new and more distant site with a new parish church, and its parishioners had the right to hold an occasional service in the Abbey church. In fact it was seldom exercised and the impression was given that it would be willingly abandoned. In the event, the legal obstacles proved insurmountable and Downside was unwilling to purchase the property with this restriction. Had today's ecumenical climate prevailed in the 30s it is unlikely that there would have been any problem.

The idea of making a new foundation had, however, become a firm policy of Abbot Chapman and he was now frequently away from Downside viewing alternative properties. Among those which were seriously considered were Wimpole House in Cambridgeshire, now a property of the National Trust, Thame Abbey near Oxford, and the Grange near Winchester. Many years later I found, as Bursar of Downside, that the memory of Abbot Chapman as a connoisseur of country estates had lingered on in many places. On Christmas Eve of this year 1932 David wrote to Outram Evennett:

> The slump of Milton has put the future once more into the melting pot. I cannot help feeling *in ossibus meis* that the next few years—four at most—will see a great sweeping away of landmarks which will leave very little that was most characteristic of external Downside before 1922.... At the same time I look forward to the future of Downside with immense and intense hope, so I am quite content that the years should bring what they may bring.

At much the same time he wrote to a friend a glowing tribute to the qualities of the Downside community, both in the natural and supernatural order (v.p. 97). All this was to change in a matter of months.

Not all members of the community shared David's confidence about the future. Milton, with its great church and roots in the medieval monastic past, had exercised an inevitable attraction for many of us, but as time passed some began to doubt if a new foundation would be directed on what seemed to many to be the right ideals. I had always been on excellent terms with the Abbot and a number of the brethren now urged me to put to him our point of view. In February 1933 we had a long talk and in a very friendly interview the Abbot admitted that he did not really know the younger members of the community or their opinions. I explained that we were anxious about the appointment of a Prior of the new foundation and he told me that he was inclined to appoint an 'oldish man' of 65 or more who would just carry things on—a spiritual leader would not be needed. Depressingly, for a young man, he added that he was a confirmed pessimist and had no wish to fight for 'causes' of any kind. A few years earlier he would have spoken differently. None of us knew at this time that he was already attacked by the disease that was to kill him in less than a year.

By May 1933 the search for a suitable estate ended with the choice of the former home, at Worth in Sussex, of Lord Cowdray, the oil magnate. The conventual Chapter voted for its purchase, but the opposition to the project represented quite a section of the resident community. Their views were based on the need to give more attention to the dependent Priory at Ealing and to the fear that a second dependency would not be given the right direction. Four months or so earlier, as we have seen, David had expressed his immense hope for the future and his contentment that the years might bring whatever was in store. All this was changed. At the Chapter he argued that the spiritual condition and observance of the community did not justify a new foundation. These views were new and extreme and I for one could not follow him in agreement. The Chapter also voted for the surrender of three parishes.

I was away from Downside after the Chapter and on my return I found that an unexpected, and to me unwelcome, development had occurred. On the one hand the Abbot had reacted strongly and publicly against those who had expressed opposition at the Chapter, and two young members of the community had discussed with David a plan for a foundation of their own which two or three others would support. He decided to lead this group and justified his action by the claim that life at Downside was incompatible with his religious profession, to accept the *status quo* would be to deny his vows. It will be remembered that only a few months earlier he had claimed that the contemplative life was possible at Downside and he was now, following a foundation at Worth, being asked to express that trust in the future which he had recently expressed. Now, although nothing in our life had changed, he claimed that Downside did not provide the framework of a monastic life in which the individual could persevere alone. At the time I found this point of view both unexpected and incomprehensible. The standard of our liturgical life was very high and, as David had written a few months earlier, as a community we had been 'extraordinarily blessed by God' in the supernatural order. Moreover the community was a tolerant one and the individual monk was free to avoid anything that he considered a distraction from the purpose of his religious life. David himself was in this respect in a privileged position. He did not teach in the school or serve a local village church. Moreover, the Abbot had served half his term of office and a more positive policy might be hoped for from a successor. The proposed foundation of Worth was condemned by David before it got under way but in the event, influenced no doubt by the opposition expressed at the Chapter, the Abbot appointed an excellent Prior and the Priory maintained a good standard of observance with daily sung Mass, Vespers and Compline, and a fairly austere daily régime. It is difficult to explain the sudden change in David's outlook, from the glowing view he held of the community and its future in 1932 to the pessimism in its regard of 1933.

David invited me for a walk in the monastery garden and told me of his plan for a foundation of his own. It came as a blow. From my novitiate days a number of us had placed much of our hope for the future on him and now he was proposing, as it seemed to me, to leave us in the lurch to face the inevitable reaction that would result from a secession. In an imperfect world one could not expect one's community to be free of all imperfection but I had never ceased to believe that the spirit of the Rule would be faithfully followed. Now I felt utterly betrayed and could offer no sympathy or support. For some of us this was to prove the end of a chapter—'never glad, confident morning again'.

Early in June David gave the Abbot a letter requesting permission to make his own foundation. This, like the proposed Worth foundation, was to include the work of a school. Some years earlier an Australian had left a large sum of money to accumulate for ten years and then to be offered to Downside for a Benedictine foundation in that country. He wished to renew the Downside connection with Australia that had begun in 1832 with the landing of Dom Bernard Ullathorne as Vicar-General and had ended in 1883 with the death of Dom Bede Vaughan, Archbishop of Sydney. A decision would have to be made about this bequest in four years' time. Now David and four others asked permission to undertake this work and their motives were explained in the letter for the Abbot: 'We would wish to do this as Downside's work, following our Constitutions to the letter and the spirit, renewing the Gregorian connexion with Australia and giving it the Benedictine life just a century after Ullathorne's landing there.' The signatories were also moved by the conviction that

> Downside had not yet realised the full stature of a monastic house in matters of poverty, regularity, and the common life. . . . It had always been our hope, till very recently, that Downside was moving . . . in the direction pointed out to us in our novitiate.
>
> Since the Chapter you have given us to understand, in public and in private . . . that our principles, our ideals, our hopes are not those of Downside, are in fact false.

The letter ended with a claim that the views of the five who signed it

> respond to the deepest, if unformulated aspirations of many, perhaps a majority of the community actually resident at Downside. We should certainly claim for them, most jealously, that they are nothing novel or strange, but are the true development in our day of what we have learnt from the greatest and holiest Gregorians of the past.

This proposal to found a monastery and school in Australia was not in itself unreasonable or opposed in any way to the Downside tradition and had not the community already committed itself to a new foundation would have received considerable support. A decision about the Australian bequest was not required for four more years and the group were prepared to wait. A wise Abbot might therefore have expressed sympathy and understanding with the knowledge that a decision could be postponed, and in the hope that satisfactory progress of the Worth foundation might prove the fears expressed to be groundless.

Unfortunately Abbot Chapman was in no fit state of health to handle the matter rationally. He sent Father David a lecture on monastic duty claiming, and in this he was in error, that the community supported his view:

> Here is a party of young men who dare—and with the air of doing something praiseworthy and holy—to say things which violate the fundamental teachings we received in our noviti- ate and have tried to act on since. . . . I wish to hear from you first, that you accept and hold the doctrine of St Benedict concerning humility and obedience and abnegation of the will . . . secondly, an explanation of how it has come to pass that you have seemed to deny it by your action.

In July the Abbot entered a London nursing home and there for the moment controversy rested.   ·

A rapid change had occurred in David's outlook since his praise of the community written in 1932. Within a few days of handing his Australian proposal to the Abbot his thoughts underwent another sudden change and he circu- lated a paper to his four followers: 'Until a week ago I had always assumed almost as an axiom that a Benedictine monastery in England must have some considerable active work—either a school or fairly widespread apostolic work . . . quite suddenly I find that gone.' He now proposed to abandon the Australian project in favour of a purely con- templative foundation in England and a scheme was put forward in some detail. He suggested that a house should be obtained in the East Anglian countryside and the adventure financed by relations and friends of the founders. The work of the community must be compatible with a life of prayer, and therefore such as could be possible within a monastic enclosure. 'A foundation made from Downside', he wrote, 'would naturally endeavour to carry on, at least in a small way, the precious Gregorian tradition of scholarship and culture, and there are some of our group who could study, write, and teach theology.' For others there would be agricultural and garden work, and Retreats might be given for guests who came to stay. All members of the community would take their share of housework and take regular exercise in field work. There would be no lay servants. The monks would rarely leave the enclosure except to give Retreats to enclosed religious of other communities. No parochial work would be undertaken.

More than ten years ago a reviewer commented on David's 'dissent from the still strong idea of his elders and many contemporaries that the monastic ideal lay in the life of a Bec, whose stress was on a long liturgical round and on scholarship. He insisted, on the contrary, that the ideal lay in the desert.' This suggests a self-conscious view of monasticism wholly alien to the Downside of the 1920s and 30s and it is incorrect to imply that David at this time was seeking 'the desert' for himself and his followers. The life he planned for his contemplative foundation was one that closely resembled that of the Congregation of France although it was to follow the Constitutions of the English Congregation. It was to be a life of simplicity and community, and possessions were not to be such as might give the impression of a comfortable life. It was to be a life of silence, except at the common recreation, but not a life of Cistercian silence. The community was to exist for those 'called by God to the contemplative life, that is to say a way of life whose chief occupation is the love and adoration of God in prayer, public and private'. Finally it was accepted that until the house could become autonomous, and this would largely depend on recruitment and financial stability, it would remain under the jurisdiction of the Abbot of Downside. Should it fail, the community would return to the mother house.

To what extent was this scheme for a contemplative foundation visionary rather than practical? A strictly contemplative community did not exist within the English Congregation, but the way of life proposed was quite compatible with its constitutions. It was not laid down that a community must have a school or do parochial work, or any other specific form of activity. Promises of financial help were secured, but this aspect of the project does not seem to have been thought out in detail. Five members would barely suffice but the number interested eventually reached nine. All were younger than David and so he could write of them as *pueri mei*. Six were priests and three more were in simple or temporary vows. Two were outstanding intellectually. It was the youth of the group which aroused misgiving in others who were not unsympathetic. I felt at the time, and my impression was confirmed later, that some members of this group were quite unsuited to a wholly contemplative life and would not have persevered. How also would David have reacted if the Abbot had promised support but on condition that he should appoint its first Superior? In retrospect it seems very doubtful if the experiment would have succeeded, but it is sad that a trial period was not permitted.

During these difficult days David had received sympathy and understanding from the Headmaster, Dom Sigebert Trafford, and it was he who read the detailed plan to the Abbot when he returned in August from the nursing home. Dom Sigebert sent David an account of the Abbot's reaction:

> I had a very lengthy talk with him in the morning and he seemed reasonable and quiet ... and finally got to the point that although not agreeing, if he could not persuade you all to

give up your ideas, then he would have to let you try, and do
his best to help you. But he added that he would like to talk to
one of the community. I saw him again in the afternoon. I
don't know whether he had seen the other member of the
community, but his whole attitude had changed. . . . I tried to
quiet him, but he only got more excited, and I had to leave
him in that frame of mind as I had to get off to catch my
train. . . . As you know, it is the youth of some of the members
that has been my doubt all along. I can only repeat again, as
I told the Abbot, that on personal grounds I don't want it to
happen, but if all are really determined about it and feel they
want a life they cannot hope for at Downside, then I think
they ought to have the opportunity. If it is a call from God
then the difficulties will melt away and nothing is going to
stop it.

A few days later David received a note from the Abbot
rejecting his proposal and refusing further discussion.
This was followed by a second letter:

I do not want to keep you in unnecessary suspense. I think it
impossible that you should remain at present at Downside as
a 'storm centre'. For the sake of peace I am very sorry to say
you must be elsewhere. I have written to the Abbot Primate
to ask whether a professor is still needed at Sant' Anselmo or
S. Paolo. I understand you are going to Stanbrook on Monday; please do not return to Downside but go on to Ealing,
until I can write to you about your future. I shall be glad to
have a talk with you before you go to Stanbrook.

A few weeks later the Abbot explained his attitude more
fully:

It has been clear ever since the chapter of May 28 that you
are regarded by a number of the younger monks as their
leader. There can be no excuse for such a party in any monastery, except where the Church gives the right to the Chapter
to decide on a matter proposed by the Abbot. Those whom
you have led have lost their loyalty to Downside, to which
they were bound by their solemn vows, and thus have put

their religious vocation in very serious jeopardy. I have told
you again and again that I do not accuse you of any theological fault, because you seem to have acted in ignorance of
monastic principles. I do not intend any punishment by
removing you from Downside.

By then he had also written to the Abbot Primate in
Rome:

Therefore the first thing is to remove Father David from
Downside. I do not think he would do harm elsewhere. He is
very pious and quiet and regular. His fault is that he cannot
see that humility and obedience come before ascetic and mystical ideals. I should be very glad to send him as a professor
at Sant' Anselmo; an alternative suggested would be St
Paul's.

It is an indication of Abbot Chapman's misjudgement
that he had in fact no power to send one of his monks to a
post outside the work of the community without the
monk's prior consent. David himself wished to become
chaplain to the nuns of Stanbrook Abbey and assured the
Abbot that he would not lead them astray by preaching
his own theories on the monastic life. His suggestion was
vetoed by the Lady Abbess who did not wish to accept a
chaplain who was involved in controversy with his abbot.
The Abbot Primate also felt unable to receive David at
Sant' Anselmo until the matter of the foundation was
settled and he therefore remained at Ealing Priory. In
November the Abbot died.

Abbot Chapman's monastic training, after his years at
Oxford, had been received in the Belgian Abbey of
Maredsous, which was at that time a house of the German
Congregation of Beuron. The tradition of this Congregation was one that tended to exalt the abbatial authority,
and this may have influenced his own conception of the
office, which tended to be authoritarian. Abbot Chapman
himself had been one of nature's rebels and it is curious
that he was so disconcerted when he in his turn encoun-

tered opposition. David and all the members of his little
group shared a love of Downside and its community and,
given sympathy and understanding, the story of their
movement might well have followed a very different
course. They certainly believed that Abbot Chapman had
called on them to reject the ideal of the monastic life at
Downside with which they had been inspired by Abbot
Ramsay and their Novice Master. Had David not been
removed from the Abbey at this time it is unlikely that he
would have left the community, as he once remarked to
me in his old age. Abbot Chapman's handling of the affair
was unfortunate in the extreme but he was, during the
critical months, stricken down by a disease which so soon
proved fatal. In November 1933, on hearing of the Abbot's
death, David wrote to his cousin, Dame Katharine Loxton:

> I cannot say too soberly or too strongly that the ultimate
> controversy was over a fragment of God's truth where there
> could be no yielding and where only one could be right. (I am
> speaking of course of the difference as it existed long before
> the idea of a foundation had come into the minds of any of
> us.) As regards the methods, ways, occasions—them, where
> human, fallible, sinful beings are concerned there is plenty of
> room for both of us to be at fault, and here I acknowledge
> entirely how much I have been to blame and more to blame,
> if you wish, solely to blame. But that I am sure he pardons
> now. ... Don't think or speak of a quarrel. My real sadness
> was more than two years ago, when I realised that never
> again—short of a miracle—would any full sympathy be poss-
> ible. How can we fear when we have been thus led so mar-
> vellously.

Chapter Six

EXILE AND 'MONASTICISM OF THE SOUL'

The ultimate controversy was over a fragment of God's truth where there could be no yielding and where only one could be right.

D. K. to K. L., 1934

The community of Ealing Priory, of which David now found himself a member, numbered some fourteen monks in 1933, and was engaged in the work of a parish and a school with both boarders and day-boys. A handsome church provided the setting for daily recital of the choral Office. David shared in the church duties but without a commitment to the parish, and with some reluctance taught a few classes in the school. This was not a heavy load and it was no hindrance to continuation of the historical studies begun at Downside in 1929. He joined the London Library and began to use the Reading Room of the British Library. He had stayed at the Priory several times in the past and had once sent me an amusing account of a Retreat he had given to a London community of nuns:

I am in the midst of my Retreat and quite enjoying it, in the moments when I don't feel the hypocrisy of talking religion to old ladies who had been in vows twenty years before I was born. Most of them are deaf and sit around me wearing the most preposterous trumpets or else not trying and dropping gently into slumber—a usual effect of my words it seems. The brethren here are very edifying, as you have always remarked. The sight of Abbot Butler reading nocturn lessons is poignant in the extreme, and Dom Dunstan [Pontifex], *pontifex maximus natus* though he be, is exemplary in his attendance in choir, in spite of his parish.

This was in happier days, and David would not have expected to become a member of the Ealing community. His parting from Downside, with its high standard of liturgical life and its large community, was painful and for a lover of the countryside life in London was a real deprivation. The Ealing community welcomed him most charitably but was unable to understand his point of view and in any case contained none of his close friends. He had now dropped out of the mainstream of life at Downside and to some extent out of mind. He had not been re-elected to the Council at the autumn Chapter. Downside was understandably preoccupied with its new foundation in Sussex where community life began with sung Vespers on the eve of Michaelmas. Many of David's friends formed part of the new Worth community, and I had been sent there to teach Church History to the young theologians while waiting to take the *viva* examinations for my doctorate at Munich. David would have been happier at Worth but Abbot Chapman had felt that his influence on a young community had to be avoided.

In December he faced the uncertainty about his future which resulted from the Abbot's death. At first it was his intention that he and his followers should not vote at the coming abbatial election and I wrote to protest at this decision. He replied on 1 December:

I liked your letter very much, and also that you should have written at all under the circumstances. I agree with all you say.... For a moment I did waver, on this argument: that I had refused to be voted for by a large number of different people of very different political opinions, and it was not

justifiable for me to vote, especially when a vote might turn
the scale and also when I did not hope myself to support
whom I voted for. . . . Again many thanks for your letter.
Always write to me if you think I am acting wrongly.

After his election the new Abbot, Dom Bruno Hicks,
wrote to David suggesting that he should go to Rome and
discuss his project there. David replied:

It was most kind of you to write so soon. . . . Believe me the
last few months have been a real agony to me—to be at
cross-purposes with one's abbot is a real agony, a night-
mare. . . . It is very kind of you to suggest that I should go out
to Rome. I know that you will realise that I love and always
have loved Downside far too much to do anything willingly
that could hurt her. . . . It has never been our intention to
break away from Downside by the suggested foundation, and
our hope was (and is) for it to be under the full jurisdiction of
the Abbot of Downside and if it did not succeed to be
absorbed back into Downside.

The journey to Rome was made shortly before Christmas, and on Christmas Day David wrote to me from Sant'
Anselmo with nostalgic thoughts of home:

It is almost impossible as I write to imagine that at Downside
the Christmas holidays are running their wonted course—
with crib, long drawn out teas in the half light of the fire,
whole holidays on the Mendips, evenings in the refectory.
Impossible—and yet all too possible to imagine.

Ich schau' dich an, und Wehmut
Schleicht mir ins Herz hinein

At Sant' Anselmo he won over to some extent the Abbot
Primate and found a quite unexpected ally in the Archbishop of Malta, a Benedictine of the English Congregation. When the Abbot of Downside arrived they persuaded
him to take a benevolent view. A letter from David to
Outram Evennett gives a full account of the proceedings:

... We discovered that the most influential person at Rome in our matter was the Primate and everyone agreed that the Congregation of Religious would refer back to him—and as he was very kind and obviously wanted to find a solution out of court we spent a fortnight in pourparlers with him and got into touch with other people.... Then the Abbot came out and the Primate had long talks with him over three days. Then the Archbishop of Malta arrived and was our most staunch friend. Then the Primate and the Abbot proposed to us (most unexpectedly) that we should go out as a body to start a contemplative house in Uganda or India—the Holy Father's approval was to be asked *instanter* and all permissions were guaranteed. We answered (after thought and prayer) that it was not the vocation we felt ourselves called to, that we had no mandate to speak for the others, that practical difficulties seemed insurmountable. After our reply negotiations broke down altogether and there was a terrible twelve hours in which all seemed lost and it looked like appealing to the Holy See against both Abbot and Primate. At this point the Archbishop of Malta did much to save us. The suggestion was made to the Abbot that an English bishop should appeal to him to make a foundation of the type desired in his diocese. The Abbot (who I think in his heart dreaded the prospect of our coming home to roost) rather unexpectedly jumped at this, and both the Archbishop and the Primate accepted it with alacrity. The Primate by this time was all for us and treated us most kindly. So thus the matter was arranged and I was to get at the Bishop of Northampton.... We are not out of the wood yet, as the thing has to come before the Council and the Chapter, but you will see that we have made progress more than I ever hoped in so short a time.... When we come to E. Anglia we shall expect a visit.

This letter suggested a confidence which in the event was ill founded. Abbot Hicks was by no means a strong character and seems to have succumbed against his better judgement to the persuasions of the Abbot Primate and the Archbishop. Back at Downside he did not give a strong lead to the Council and the proposal was rejected by a decisive majority. It was unfortunate for David at this juncture that he had failed to secure re-election to that body at the previous autumn Chapter. The Abbot had, however, at some stage made an alternative offer. It so happened that Downside served the parish of Beccles, in East Anglia, where there was a fine church with a large house attached, and it was suggested that David and his followers should establish an experimental community there.

This offer was rejected on the ground that one member of the small community would have to minister to the parish and this would be incompatible with the aims of a totally contemplative community. In spite of David's statement that he wished his foundation to be under the Abbot's jurisdiction he did not really trust him to leave such a community free to establish itself, and did not wish his community to be under close scrutiny from Downside. On the visit to Rome David had been accompanied by one of the brethren who, as a former officer in the Guards and ADC to a Governor of Malta, had some experience of negotiation. He had been distressed by his leader's rigid attitude and lack of finesse in all these negotiations. By April 1934 it was decided to petition Rome, and when David wrote to inform Abbot Hicks of this decision he added: 'Whatever answer Rome might give us as to our own future we would trust in God that he would give us grace to obey fully and frankly.' In the previous December the Abbot Primate had commented with foresight: 'I doubt very much whether a decision of the Holy See will be able to bring their minds to rest.'

It so happened that in May of this year, having completed my examinations at Munich, I journeyed on to Rome to research for a brief period in the Vatican Library. I heard from David before leaving:

> It was very pleasant to hear from you after such a long silence of us both—a silence long on my part only because it is wellnigh impossible to discuss, save face to face, the subject which has been my one interest for so many months. . . . I have heard no word from Rome. If while you are there either

the Primate or Dom Langdon [Procurator in Curia] speak to you *de re nostra* I would only beg you *ex memoria veteris amicitiae* to correct any information that may have been inaccurately given, and to leave to the Lord, so far as may be, the direction of all else. I somehow feel we shall not ever find ourselves together in permanence again.... But I hope we may meet somewhere in the summer. You might give a dinner to celebrate your doctorate!

I was not to know at the time, but this letter marked the beginning of a break in our correspondence which was to last for nearly twenty years.

The petition had been forwarded to Dom Philip Langdon so that he might transmit it to the Congregation of Religious. It was signed by six priests and also by four Junior monks, none of the four being in solemn vows. The petition claimed that Downside could not provide the framework for a wholly monastic and contemplative life. According to the procedure obtaining at that time it had little chance of success, for the Congregation of Religious at once returned it to the Procurator and invited his opinion. Dom Philip was entirely opposed to the project of a contemplative foundation but in any case, as a monk of another community, would have found it difficult to take a line of his own against the wishes of the Abbot of Downside. In June 1934 the Congregation issued a rescript rejecting the petition and it urged the signatories to continue to live as perfectly as they could in the monastery of their profession. This decision was immediately accepted by all except David. In July he wrote to the Abbot: 'I cannot however believe that the matter has been placed sufficiently clearly and fully before the Holy Father.... Therefore I intend to have the whole matter represented to the Holy Father by someone who has a full understanding of the issue at stake.'

He was then told that the Abbot Primate had raised the matter once more in an audience with the Pope, but he still persisted in his view: 'The real motive of our request

was never really understood or discussed at all in
Rome. . . . We are all of us ready to go through with the
time of testing.'

In this last belief David was mistaken. The Abbot considered his attitude to be reprehensible and the tone of the
letters he received now showed a significant change. In
one letter David wrote of the Abbot's unwillingness 'to
seek the truth and nothing but the truth' and rejected an
offer of a meeting: 'All discussion of the matter between us
when you are here next week would be worse than waste of
time, and I do not intend that it shall be discussed.' It is
from this point on that a tone of 'infallibility' can be noted
in his letters with their severe judgements on others. Thus
in November he wrote to one of his closest collaborators in
the foundation movement: 'You are in darkness, and
rightly so, since you are wholly occupied with what is not
God.'

He had refused to accept that his followers had all submitted to the Roman decision and to one Junior who had
decided to begin a fresh novitiate in a French monastery
he wrote: 'You should have awaited my words. Your soul
has been given to me by God, and nothing that you can do
will ever take it from my hands.' He now sent out a
remarkable document to all his former associates:

> If we are in future to go together to God, you must decide the
> following:
>   1 to submit to me and to me alone any decision that relates
> to your inner life either directly (i.e. your soul's life) or indi-
> rectly (i.e. our common future)
>   2 to seek spiritual advice from no outsider
>   3 when your daily external task of obedience is accomp-
> lished to withdraw from all that is superfluous into silence
> and recollection
>   4 Finally if you cannot . . . fulfill these conditions you
> have NO vocation to the contemplative life. I will proceed if
> need be alone.

In fact the group had now broken up. Seven remained in

the Downside community, of whom one was later to become Novice Master, a post he held for twelve years. Two Juniors in simple vows went through a second novitiate at Solesmes and were solemnly professed for Quarr Abbey; a third was to be ordained to the secular priesthood but later returned to Downside. David was left alone, irreconcilable and withdrawn.

At first he kept in touch with old friends and visited Sligger Urquhart before he died, writing of this visit to Outram Evennett:

> It was pleasant—no, more than pleasant, edifying in the real sense—to see and hear of the real devotion shown to Urquhart in his last weeks at Balliol. Quite apart from the Master's giving an invalid the use of his house and Cyril Bailey's obituary, both Humphrey Sumner and Roger Mynors waited upon him like sons, and showed real *pietas* and grief. . . . One hears so much of academic spite and pettiness that it was a real joy to see such charity, worthy of a religious community, at Balliol.

Gradually, however, he began to avoid social contacts and to sever the ties of friendship. He avoided visitors when they came to the Priory, and to Evennett he gave an explanation:

> I acted as I did three years ago in order that I might live, according to the monastic vocation, in that solitude— primarily spiritual, but also of necessity physical—which has always been and must be, a part of the true monastic life . . . and that is why, gradually, I have withdrawn from all that is not part of the work that obedience calls me to do . . . come to Ealing still, but not to see me as in the past.

At the community gathering after a meal he now sat apart, not speaking unless spoken to, and for a small and charitable community this was distressing, for all without exception had hoped to see him fully integrated into the common life. It was an attitude which he would himself have condemned in earlier days but it was one indication that he was psychologically in a disturbed condition. It is possible to wonder why his superiors took no action about this self-imposed isolation but it was masked by the devotion with which David fulfilled his monastic duties.

During this year, to an extent unrealised by the community, David had come under a new influence which was to determine his future. In February 1934 the Prior of Ealing had asked him to interview a medical student named Elizabeth Kornerup who had asked for spiritual direction. She was of Swedish nationality, and a fairly recent convert to Catholicism from Lutheranism. When she qualified as a doctor she specialised in psychiatry and worked for a time at the Tavistock Clinic. David was greatly impressed by her when they met. Elizabeth Kornerup was deeply interested in the spiritual life, had taken a vow of chastity, and followed the teaching of his favourite St John of the Cross. She on her part showed great interest and encouraged him in his plans for a contemplative foundation, while he felt that he was in the presence of a very holy person, in fact a saint. This proved to be the beginning of a lifelong friendship and he saw her regularly. It was a friendship which he wished to share with his followers and one by one, as occasion offered, they were introduced to her. Some were equally impressed but not all. In a letter to Abbot Hicks one of his closest followers mentioned her effect on Father David:

> He at once received such an impression of her holiness that he took her completely into his confidence with regard to the projected foundation. Henceforth they both believed that she had been sent to him by God in order to help forward this cause. . . . He grew in the belief that she was a perfect soul and a saint.

Later he wrote again: 'Father David has now to my certain knowledge given her the Last Sacraments four times. . . . He told me that on important Feastdays her

spiritual life becomes so intense that her body cannot
stand the strain.'

The Jesuit, Father Steuart, had some dealings with her
and formed no favourable impression, while two eminent
psychiatrists gave conflicting opinions. One, a Catholic,
wrote to the Abbot and stated that she was 'a colleague of
excellent repute', but the other judged her a very unbal-
anced person and 'ultra religious'. Without doubt she was
a remarkable and able woman who was convinced of the
rightness of her actions, and believed that she had a mis-
sion to protect David and assist him with his plans. It
would seem that the normal role of spiritual director and
penitent became reversed and that she assumed the
dominant role, so that David sought her advice before
taking action concerning himself or his relations with
Downside. Following her guidance he began to give up all
external contacts and engagements. He came to believe
that his primary duty as a priest, above all else, was to
protect what he felt was her God-given life. The spiritual
life of Elizabeth Korr erup was certainly unusual: she went
to confession every day and had a different confessor for
every day of the week, since a regular confessor would not
have permitted this practice. She carried always with her
a consecrated Host, received the anointing of the sick
regularly, and spent long hours in prayer.

In letters to his little band of followers David referred to
her as Sister Elizabeth or Sister Bridget, a reference to St
Bridget of Sweden. She is mentioned in May 1934 in his
account of a meeting with the Carmelite Prioress of Notting Hill. The latter had become very well known, largely
because she had founded more Carmelite convents in England than St Teresa of Avila had done in sixteenth-century
Spain. David had called at a convent near Cambridge
with one of his supporters and the Superior introduced the
Prioress of Notting Hill:

> We could see that it was an old nun, and I wondered for a
> moment if the Prioress was getting off Mother Melchisedech

on us while she did something else. Then she spoke: 'I am the
old Mother of Notting Hill. I have heard for some time what
you are doing, and I have come to tell you I am praying very
much for it' . . . Isn't it just how He [Our Lord] works: He
doesn't give the immediate thing you want (abbot's consent
or what not) but throws at your head something you would
never have prayed for, like Sister [Elizabeth] and this.

Other letters to one of his followers are revealing:

Last night Sr Bridget came and I told her all—or rather she
asked me until she knew all. Her advice so struck in with my
deepest conviction—with the truth of God and after all she is
a *perfect* soul—that I shall do my best to take it. She said, in
effect, that we must be prepared for complete *apparent* failure,
and if necessary every kind of hostility. . . . She says 'Father
Abbot so far is blind. We must surround him with love on
Friday' . . . I speak quite literally when I say she is a *perfect*
soul, so you will understand what it means when I say that
although she is seriously ill she is going to fast on Friday on
water alone—no food—to give strength to her prayers—
which of course are not prayers but *ascensus mentis in Deum*.

He wrote again:

You can imagine talking to such a soul is a perpetual leap in
the dark. Only because of *my* faith does *hers* seem real to me,
and then I have in the light of *hers* to sanction conduct which
reason would condemn as fantastic—and then, when the
doubt comes 'who are you, so utterly imperfect and
unspiritual, to deal in things like this—what if it is all one
great delusion—yours, hers?' Only I know—or try to hold by
faith—that it is not.

Again a week later: ' . . . if Sister Elizabeth were released
for the Press I simply dare not think what reception would
be accorded to her. . . . Unless one has seen in action, so to
say, a perfect soul, one just has no idea of what perfection
is. The *strength* necessary.'

Meanwhile Abbot Hicks had to undergo a severe opera-
tion and continued ill health led to his resignation of the
abbacy in 1938; in his place Dom Sigebert Trafford was
elected in December. The new Abbot's relations with
David had always been most friendly and he had given
support and sympathy to his plans for a contemplative
foundation. David had appreciated this support and in
February of this year had written to one of his followers:
'Our great helper, to whom we owe more than we can say,
is R.S.T. . . . He is doing all he can for us.' Abbot Trafford's first thought was to bring David back into the main
community, and he wrote at once asking him to come to
Downside. It was an affectionate letter, but David con-
sulted Dr Kornerup and refused the Abbot's request.
Abbot Trafford was prepared to go himself to meet him,
either at Ealing or anywhere in London but all his
attempts met with refusal. Later he was to record that
'from the very first day of my becoming Abbot he has
refused to have any contact with me.'

This was an impossible situation. During 1939 David
seemed to his brethren in the Priory to be living in a state
of great strain and tension, a totally observant monk in his
daily life, but refusing to have any relationship with his
Abbot. How different this state of things was from the
letter of 1928 in which he had written to me: 'I hate the
feeling of differing from an abbot, simply because he is
abbot *et vices Christi creditur agere in monasterio.*'

The outbreak of war brought this impossible state of
things to an end in September. David secured permission
from the Prior to be away for one night and left the Priory
never to return. His departure seemed to be unpremedi-
tated and he left his personal effects and papers behind,
but it seems to have been planned by Dr Kornerup who
had recently acquired the tenancy of a flat above hers
where David was now to live. One of the Ealing monks
visited him at this address and sent an account to the
Abbot:

My impression from start to finish was that he is not in a normal state of mind; he seemed hypnotised and without will or thought of his own. His manner was dull and listless; his only answer to everything was that the doctor was giving him a course of treatment as an invalid and he had entrusted himself entirely to her care and management. He had read no letters, but had given her permission to open and deal with all. She was dealing with him for you, as he was an invalid. He could not be in rebellion, for an invalid could not rebel. . . . If this is a true estimate of his state, it would seem that he cannot be proceeded against as a rebellious subject. It is pathetic to see such a fine mind and spirit brought to this.

By temperament Abbot Trafford was the last man to remain passive in this situation and he was convinced that if only they could meet all would be well. Yet all his letters to David suggesting a meeting were returned by Dr Kornerup with a statement that her patient was not fit to deal with correspondence. The Abbot decided to visit David at his new address without advance warning, and he took with him Dr Bradley of the Ministry of Health who, as one-time resident medical officer at Downside, had known David's past medical history. As a result of this meeting it was agreed that David should visit a well-known consultant psychiatrist although neither the Abbot nor Dr Bradley was convinced that he was mentally ill. At the time it was agreed that the report should be sent to the Abbot, but in the event Dr Kornerup telephoned the consultant to request that the report should not be sent to him. In fact the psychiatrist had already given Abbot Trafford his opinion by telephone and had advised that David should leave Dr Kornerup's care. This he refused to do.

By taking up residence outside the monastery without permission David had thereby incurred the penalties of canon law: he was *ipso facto* excommunicated and his *celebret*, or permission to celebrate Mass, was withdrawn. He now refused, on the ground of illness, to recognise these penalties and appealed to the Abbot President, writing that it was his wish 'to proceed in all ways constitutionally within our Congregation'. The Procurator in Curia, Dom Philip Langdon, who was in England at this time, travelled to London at David's request for a discussion. On arrival he was given a letter asking him to see Dr Kornerup instead, which he refused to do. However, another official of the Congregation saw her in late October and was told that she had for some time recognised symptoms of schizophrenia, partly a result of disappointment over the projected foundation. She showed him the consultant's report and expressed her belief that David was seriously ill. An account of this meeting was sent to Abbot Trafford: 'Throughout he spoke slowly, seemed dazed and over-tired; repeatedly said he was ill and could not think. If he was acting it was extraordinarily good acting—I was disposed to think it was not acting.'

It was now agreed that a second consultant opinion should be obtained and this time a Catholic psychiatrist was called in, a man of eminent standing in his profession. In January 1940 he diagnosed a nervous breakdown and a mild case of schizophrenia. At first he was inclined to let David 'hibernate', as he put it, in the care of Dr Kornerup but when she decided to give up his medical care he offered to drive David down to a nursing home outside London.

Meanwhile Abbot Trafford had at last received an encouraging letter from David which ended: 'I would like to say at once that it is my desire to give you as my lawful superior the humble submission which I owe, and to return to the monastery when my health permits.' The Abbot replied that all would be well if he would accept the psychiatrist as his medical attendant and act on his advice. This was ill received for what David was seeking was an immediate permission to celebrate Mass again, whereas the Abbot would give this only after he had left the care of Dr Kornerup. At this point David decided that the consultant was under Abbot Trafford's influence and refused to accept him as his medical adviser. Early in

March 1940 the Abbot wrote again to David, the last of twelve letters in all:

'Could I meet you. Never a day goes by but what I think of you and pray for you.' A meeting was refused and after an official warning of the consequences it was recorded at Downside that he had left the community; he was not formally dismissed but his name was removed from the list of members. In April David replied to the Abbot's letter which informed him of this decision: 'Your last letter to me was, as you know, inspired not by any love of the monastic life, which you have never lived, nor by respect for canon law, of which you know nothing.'

From now on David held to the view that he had been treated with complete injustice and never ceased to resent the removal of his name from the list of the community. Yet as opinion stood in 1940 it was not possible to permit a monk to remain as a patient in the house of a woman doctor against the advice of a consultant psychiatrist. When a new Abbot wished, in 1947, to regularise David's canonical status Dr Kornerup warned him that on matters concerning Downside 'his mind cannot function normally'. A Jesuit intermediary who had several long talks with him noticed this also and in January 1949 wrote:

> I am still in uncertainty as to the agonising question of how far he is unbalanced. How can one reconcile the idea of a clouded mind with the vivid clarity not only of his achievement as a professor but with ... his setting forth of his self defence over the one issue of the validity of his rejection.... The alternative view that he is set in obstinate pride, it does not seem to fit.

David desired reinstatement but also demanded an admission that he had been unjustly treated. He wrote to the Procurator in Curia: 'To make even a token submission of the justice of the punitive action taken against me in 1939–40 would be to act against truth and conscience.' When it seemed that agreement might be reached, the Abbot of Downside wrote to him: 'If you write to me recognising my authority and name any priest with whom I may communicate I can authorise him to take the necessary steps [i.e. absolution from the canonical censures incurred in 1939]. Do you wish exclaustration or permission to reside outside the monastery?' He received an uncompromising reply: 'Downside does not observe the Rule either in the letter or the spirit, still less the Gospel teaching upon which the Rule depends. . . . I cannot in conscience ask for absolution from faults which I am not conscious of having committed.'

Yet at this same time he published in the *Journal of Theological Studies* a sensitive obituary notice of a member of the community which seemed to contradict the denunciation of Downside. Of Dom Hugh Connolly he wrote that those who had known him would recall an example 'of mental discipline and exact scholarship; and they will recall his unaffected simplicity, his sincerity, and the lowliness of heart with which he walked before God. His was the *umbratica vita* of study and religious duty.'

At last a point was reached at which agreement seemed likely. David refused the offer of exclaustration and expressed a wish to remain a member of the community with permission to live outside the monastery. It was not perhaps a logical choice.

Three times David agreed to submit to the canonical procedure and three times drew back at the last moment. Finally in March 1951 he accepted the conditions and received permission to celebrate Mass. Now a further difficulty arose. At his request permission had been obtained from Rome for him to live outside the monastery, while remaining a member of the community. It was granted on condition that he made a brief yearly visit for a Retreat. This he now refused to do and claimed that 'to make a Retreat at Downside would be to accept the life there as fully monastic in character and to present myself as a returned prodigal.' Yet he had refused the alternative of exclaustration which would have freed him of this obligation. The Downside authorities had shown remarkable patience through all these hesitations, which had endured for over three years, but now decided to withdraw and ask the Roman Congregation of Religious to impose its own solution. In October 1952 the Congregation declared that David was exclaustrated and a rescript to this effect was sent to him from Rome by the Abbot Primate. In reply Dr Kornerup wrote that the rescript was unacceptable and had not been read by David on grounds of health; he was, however, aware of its contents and told the Bishop of Northampton that he regarded it as invalid. David delayed the use of his permission to say Mass until Lady Day 1957, partly because he was reluctant to make known his absolution from censure and partly because he desired some explicit sign of a change of heart from the Abbot of Downside.

This ended the unhappy story of David's period in the ecclesiastical wilderness; his status as a Catholic priest was fully restored, and from then on he felt able to meet individual members of the Downside community on a friendly footing. Canonically he was an exclaustrated monk and the Abbot Primate had explained that the Roman decision 'does not excommunicate you from the monastery and from the right to spiritual privileges'; when he died he would be prayed for exactly as any other member of the community, but he was now under the jurisdiction of the diocesan Bishop, and not under that of his Abbot. To the end of his life he regarded himself as a monk. In a brief exposition of monastic teaching published many years before, he had written: 'Neither habit nor choir nor community life are essential to sanctity and a life of prayer. If the end of all monastic observance, the monasticism of the soul, be once attained, it may be retained no matter where one is.'

It will have been noted that in 1932–3 his views had swung rapidly from a belief that the contemplative life could be lived at Downside in an admirable community to the view that its observance was unsatisfactory; from the project to found a monastery and school in Australia to a

sudden determination to found a purely contemplative
house in East Anglia. If this might seem a history of incon-
sistency it can be said that after 1939 he was entirely
consistent in the harshness of his judgement of his former
community, and the strength of his resentment of what he
considered the unjust treatment of his canonical censure.
This attitude continued long after his status had been
restored. In 1966 he rebuked a friend who had given a
Retreat to the Downside community:

> What could you do for them? If you gave them the truth of
> Christian severity and the true following of our Lord they
> would not hear and be converted . . . in all seriousness, if I
> had anything to do with Downside as such, I would feel and
> feel rightly, that I had sinned against God.

It was then nearly thirty years since he had known Downside at first hand.

Here perhaps an earlier judgement on the Downside
community may be recalled. Only a few months before his
plan to found a contemplative community, he had written
very differently in 1932:

> I have felt this last year as never before what marvellous gifts
> we have to thank the Lord for here. It is impossible to analyse
> perhaps, but I would suggest. . . . On the natural human side
> we have a community which in variety and depth of gifts, and
> in abundance of charm—and in vivacity and alertness and
> piquancy—it would be hard to parallel. It is in a sense the
> Athens of English Catholicism. We have inherited from—
> Edmund Bishop, Cuthbert Butler, Ullathorne, Ramsay
> among others—a highly developed critical faculty, positive as
> well as negative, which prevents us thinking the second rate
> first rate, and which prevents anything parochial and provin-
> cial.
>
> In the supernatural order we are almost completely free
> from any cramping method or modalities of religion. Conse-
> quently the big, primary things—the tradition of theology
> and spirituality, the liturgy, the monastic past—are all there
> in their fullness for us. We may if we choose play golf instead,

but if we choose anything religious, it comes to us in a completely Catholic form. As in the order of natural gifts, so with the supernatural—we have been extraordinarily blessed by God. I have had a chance, this way and that, in the last two or three years, of seeing grace almost visibly flowering in two or three, and there are many others. And it is that ultimately that gives depth and richness.

This judgement on the community of 1932 was a verdict on a monastic house which he knew from within; that of 1966 was made on a community to which he was a stranger. In these days when triumphalism is an ugly word a monk of Downside would confirm the paneygyric of 1932 in more humble terms. Let others judge the verdict of 1966.

Chapter Seven

ACADEMIC CAREER

I had the good fortune to meet with a group, both at
Peterhouse and in the Faculty of History, of unusually
good and just men.

D. K. to A. S., 1963

In 1940 the Cambridge University Press published the
book which David had completed during his years at Ealing Priory, *The Monastic Order*. Three more years were
spent in London working on its sequel. Access to original
documents was not possible during the war years but the
Reading Room of the British Library remained open,
together with the London Library and that of the War-
burg Institute. Learned societies still held their meetings,
although numbers attending were severely depleted, and
in 1941 David began to attend the gatherings of the Royal
Historical Society and was soon elected a Fellow. The
splendid reviews which followed publication of *The Monastic Order* had placed him at once among the ranks of established historical scholars and in November he visited
Cambridge to receive the degree of Doctor of Letters, and
was presented for the degree by Z. N. Brooke of Caius
College, then Chairman of the Faculty of History. A second visit followed in 1943 when he read a paper at a
meeting of the Cambridge Historical Society. Its members
were drawn from the dons and research students who
remained at the University during the war and this visit

enabled David to meet senior historians, including the Secretary, Herbert Butterfield of Peterhouse. A year later he was elected a Fellow of the Society of Antiquaries, and on this occasion, in addition to Rose Graham, enlisted Dom Ethelbert Horne of Downside as one of his sponsors. It was not long before he was elected to the Council of the Royal Historical Society and an offer was made of an academic post. At the end of 1943 Cambridge University decided to fill the professorial chairs left vacant during the war, and Herbert Butterfield of Peterhouse was elected to the Chair of Modern History. This left a vacancy on the teaching staff of the College and Butterfield decided to propose David for the vacant Fellowship. In 1944 he was invited to visit the College and the formal offer was made and accepted.

Peterhouse was the most ancient of the colleges in the University and had been founded in the late thirteenth century by a bishop of Ely who was himself a monk. It had increased its reputation under two Masters of unusual background, Lord Chalmers and Field Marshal Lord Birdwood, and the influence of Harold Temperley and the Senior Tutor, Paul Vellacott, had given it a special reputation for history. Vellacott had later become Master of the College after a brief and not especially successful term as Headmaster of Harrow. He was a man of considerable charm whose health had suffered as a result of service in the First World War which had won him a DSO. At the time of David's election only four Fellows were in residence, and the Master and most of the Fellows were absent on war work of one kind and another. When Vellacott returned to the College at the end of the war, although David did not find it easy to establish a relationship, he soon began to appreciate him as an interesting personality, and to admire his efforts to maintain high standards of life and social behaviour in a changing world. As an undergraduate I had known Vellacott well, had enjoyed his hospitality and his dry wit.

The election of a monk to a Cambridge Fellowship was

an unusual event and reflected great credit on those responsible. David was the first priest monk to hold a Fellowship at a Cambridge college since the days of James II, and the precedent of that time was not a happy one. He was now forty-six years old, his background was a classical one, and he had had no experience of teaching history. Had the appointment been delayed a year or so there would have been many eligible and well-qualified young men available who were now serving in the war. David entered into residence for the October term of 1944. For some four years he had been leading a secluded, and in many ways difficult, life in London, deprived of work which would have brought him into contact with other people. The process of adjusting to a new life after cutting himself off from his community must have been both difficult and painful. His main task now was to supervise a dozen or so undergraduates who came to him at fixed times, and in wartime there were few social engagements. There was, however, still time for prayer, spiritual reading, and the daily breviary Office. Much of his time was given to work on *The Religious Orders in Medieval England*. His first lectures for a wider undergraduate audience took the form of a special subject for the second part of the History Tripos and for this he chose as his subject the lives of St Francis of Assisi and the early friars. He also accepted, at the request of Brian Wormald, the task of external examiner to the History sixth form at Charterhouse, a contact he enjoyed. Among those he examined there was William Rees-Mogg, future editor of *The Times*, whose home was close to Downside. It is curious that, having found his life at Downside, with its freedom from teaching and its rich liturgical life, inadequate for the life of contemplative prayer that he sought, he should now have returned to a life of teaching and lecturing minus the framework of community life.

With the end of the war the University resumed its former busy life, and those of the Peterhouse Fellows who had been absent on war service returned, among them

men of distinction. They included Keith Guthrie, the
Public Orator and a specialist in ancient philosophy, the
brilliant Denis Brogan, and Munia Postan, who returned
to the Chair of Economic History. David retained happy
memories of the Fellows of his College and perhaps judged
them more charitably than he did members of his former
community. He also enjoyed his contacts with undergraduates. Among his pupils he numbered the son of his
one-time classical master at Downside, and a former pupil
of mine. Hugh Watts was a cricket Blue who also played
for Somerset. In October 1945 a younger son of Z. N.
Brooke, Christopher, came into residence at Caius College
and a happy friendship began which led to some valuable
collaboration and lasted until David died. Promotion in
the academic hierarchy was swift. In 1946 David was
appointed to a university lectureship which gave him security of tenure, but he was destined to hold this for only a
few months. Professor Z. N. Brooke died in October of
that year and the Chair of Medieval History fell vacant.
I had been privileged to begin a collaboration with Z. N.
Brooke for an edition of the letters of Gilbert Foliot and
my memories of him as an inspiring teacher and kind
friend went back to undergraduate days. From the beginning he had been a generous friend to David and had done
much to further his academic career. David was now
elected to the vacant Chair, but acceptance involved the
loss of his Fellowship at Peterhouse as he would no longer
be permitted to undertake undergraduate supervision. A
college had to be found which would offer him a professorial Fellowship. The long-standing connection of Christ's,
his own old College, with Downside made a return there
difficult but in the event, to his own satisfaction, he was
enabled to remain at Peterhouse.

Appointment to the medieval Chair brought a widening
of interests and influence. In 1947 he examined for the first
time in the second part of the Historical Tripos and was
invited by Richard Pares to serve as an external examiner
at Edinburgh University; he was also elected to the British

Academy. The Ford Lectures of 1949 given at Oxford were subsequently published under the title of *The Episcopal Colleagues of Thomas Becket,* a useful book which has been frequently quoted by later workers in that field. In his memoir for the British Academy Professor C. N. L. Brooke commented on David's power as a lecturer, on 'the beauty of his language and the depth of his thought' which made his best lectures memorable and impressive. Two of the printed lectures give some illustration of this quality: the Raleigh Lecture on Archbishop Thomas Becket given at the British Academy and published in 1949, and the inaugural lecture as Regius Professor on *The Historian and Character* (1954.) A series of lectures which had considerable influence was given as a Special Subject for the Tripos with the title of *Medieval Intellectual Life,* but the book which resulted from them, *The Evolution of Medieval Thought*, gives no adequate impression of their importance. They attracted some of the best undergraduates of their year and inspired several of them to follow successful lines of research which in turn produced some valuable publications. David valued the series as providing an element of speculative reasoning which was in those days absent from most historical courses.

As a supervisor of research students Professor Brooke found him sparing of advice and criticism, and several other former pupils have confirmed this impression. In the one instance where I read a Ph.D. dissertation by one of his pupils I was surprised that he had not been critical of faults of presentation and style when his own standard in these matters was so high. For pupils of outstanding ability the quality of the teacher is not necessarily significant but, if in some cases David had little specialist knowledge of their chosen subject, all felt the better for contact with a scholar of his distinction and most of them remained friends for life. His first research student was Rosalind Brooke of Girton, who published work on Elias and the early Franciscans, while his second was Daniel Waley who became Keeper of the Manuscripts and Egerton Librarian at the British Library. For a year he supervised Giles Constable, sent by Helen Cam from Harvard, who in turn became an authority on medieval monasticism, and after holding the Medieval Chair at Harvard is today Head of Dumbarton Oaks. Gordon Leff researched on the late medieval English scholastics, published a Penguin on medieval thought and in due course held a personal Chair at York. Richard Vaughan, to whom David recommended Mathew Paris as a subject for research, became Professor of Medieval History at Hull; David Luscombe published a work of distinction on Abelard and is now a professor at Sheffield. After 1950 David became interested in a new venture which led to the publication of *Monastic Sites from the Air*. Through Martin Charlesworth, then Vice-Master of St John's, he had been introduced to a young Fellow of Selwyn College, Kenneth St Joseph, a scientist and geographer who had served in the RAF during the war and had become familiar with the technique of aerial photography. Charlesworth, an ancient historian, had become interested in a collection of photographs which St Joseph had made of Romano-British sites. In due course this work received recognition from both archaeologists and historians, and a grant was given by the Nuffield Foundation for its development.

Late in 1954 David became Chairman of the History Faculty Board, an office which he enjoyed, and he was fortunate in his secretaries, especially Geoffrey Elton. He served on many committees, was a member of the Council of the British Academy, of the Council of the Society of Antiquaries, and of the Royal Historical Society, of which he became President. Among other activities he included service on the Board of Management of the Institute of Historical Research and he became the first President of the Ecclesiastical History Society, which he helped to found. Professor Brooke has commented that, although he was often an effective chairman or committee member, David shrank from controversy and was not always successful in handling men who stated their opinions aggressively. For seven years he served as a Syndic of the Cambridge University Press, one of those who considered every work proposed for publication, and he enjoyed the fortnightly meetings. One morning in the year 1954 he received a letter marked 'From the Prime Minister' which contained an offer of the Regius Chair of Modern History. He thus became a successor to Lord Acton and the first Roman Catholic priest to hold the position since its foundation in the eighteenth century as a buttress of the Protestant Succession. Meanwhile, there had been a change in the Mastership of Peterhouse when Herbert Butterfield succeeded after the death of Paul Vellacott. It was to Butterfield that David owed his own call to Cambridge and he regarded him with affection as well as with admiration, as an administrator and scholar of unusual ability who had not lost his early democratic outlook.

In 1963 the time came for his own retirement from the Regius Chair and by then further honours had come his way. In 1961 he was elected to the Athenaeum under Rule II for members of distinction, and much earlier he had received an honorary Doctorate at Oxford. Thirty years earlier he had met the Vice-Chancellor, Maurice Bowra, in Sligger Urquhart's rooms at Balliol. Honorary degrees from other universities followed: Birmingham, Bristol, Kent, Leicester, London and York. Cambridge honoured him with a Doctorate of Divinity which he greatly valued. He remarked to me, however, that his only recent excursion into anything resembling theology had been a pamphlet in defence of the papal encyclical, *Humanae Vitae*, at that time under widespread criticism.

Before David left the University a ceremony took place at Peterhouse at which he was presented with a volume of his own articles entitled *The Historian and Character*. The book was subscribed by friends, colleagues and admirers, and edited by Christopher Brooke and Giles Constable. Three friends came from Oxford for the occasion: Trevor-Roper, Billy Pantin, and Beryl Smalley. It was the end of nineteen happy years and he always remained grateful for the ready welcome and the friendly relationships that he had found in the College and in the Faculty of History. He expressed these feelings in a letter to a friend:

> I made no move whatever to go to Cambridge nineteen years ago and had there no abiding city. I had the good fortune to meet with a group, both at Peterhouse and in the Faculty of History, of unusually good and just men. . . . In this I think I was exceptionally fortunate. Academics elsewhere, and in other colleges and faculties at Cambridge, are not always noted for the good qualities I met with.

Here we may recall the impression that David himself made on one academic among the Oxford historians of his time. W. A. Pantin wrote of him: 'It would be difficult to imagine anyone further removed from the combative, self-assertive, self-important personalities that are sometimes found in the academic jungle, or from the dons

> "who shout and bang and roar and bawl
> The Absolute across the hall."

In August David took farewell of his faithful 'bedder', sported his door for the last time, and handed over the keys of his rooms to the head porter of the College. During the next ten years he returned to Cambridge often; both Peterhouse and Christ's gave him an honorary Fellowship.

Throughout his years at Cambridge David had spent the vacations with Dr Kornerup and in retirement lived partly in her cottage near Liphook and partly in a house at Wimbledon. It was a curious but innocent relationship. He had never ceased to believe that it was part of his vocation as a priest to care for a 'perfect soul'; she on her side felt privileged to care for the health and comfort of a priest of his distinction. Every day at the cottage she served his Mass. There is no doubt, to my mind, that this close relationship, with its religious foundation, supplied for David the absence of the support and intimate companionship of a religious community to which he had once been accustomed. Without it he would have been, in spite of his many friends, a lonely man. He would certainly have had in mind the mutual support of many men and women evidenced in the history of the Church: of St Teresa and St John of the Cross, of St Francis of Assisi and St Clare, of St Francis de Sales and St Jane Chantal. It was a relationship which his friends came to accept without question but it was at times liable to cause misunderstanding to those who knew him less intimately. A Fellow of another college once mentioned to me his surprise at an incident he had witnessed at Peterhouse when Dr Kornerup appeared during the course of a college Feast 'to take the professor home'. Whenever I met Elizabeth Kornerup during the last year of David's life I sensed a certain pathos in her request for my agreement that he was in perfect health, as though seeking reassurance against her knowledge that time was running out for them both. It was only natural that I had deplored her influence but I could not question her devotion. She did not long outlive him.

In retirement, David's activity as a writer increased and he did not lose touch with the academic world. He gave the Sarum lectures at Oxford and delivered a memorable lecture on St John of the Cross in the Divinity School at Cambridge. Some of his current undertakings were mentioned in a letter of 1971 to Dom Alberic Stacpoole:

> I am absurdly full up at the moment largely because I received an SOS to stop a gap in the Patristic Conference at Oxford in mid September (*on the Regula Magistri*), and assembling *disjecta membra* of a memoir of Christopher Dawson for the British Academy; plus reading six or eight heavy books chosen by other members of the committee for the Collins prize for a religious book.

He was often called upon by publishers to advise on works submitted to them and to read the work of friends and former pupils. He was always generous in giving time to

young students and one of them paid tribute after his
death:

> I would testify to his immense kindness to the utterly undis-
> tinguished among young scholars unknown to him. No
> appeal for help went unanswered in the beautifully clear
> hand and the neat blue ink, and the humbler the request
> academically the kinder he was. Looking back on the letters I
> received I am astonished at his humility and capacity for
> infinite trouble.

A wide circle of friends retained their contacts with him.
Christopher Brooke was especially close to him and a
long-standing collaboration resulted in the publication of
their *Heads of Religious Houses in England and Wales 940–1216,*
which appeared from the Cambridge Press in 1972. Professor Brooke has told the story of how he left the early
lists on top of a London bus and recovered them by an
energetic pursuit through the London streets. David also
had a close friendship with that remarkable man Peter
Morrison, managing director of the publishing firm of
Thomas Nelson, who had at one time invited him to edit
the works of St Anselm. Morrison shone as the publisher
of medieval texts, including the series to which David contributed an edition of Lanfranc's *Statutes.* He made regular
visits to Kenneth Clark at Saltwood, enjoying a friendship
that had first begun in the 1920s at Sligger Urquhart's
chalet. In his autobiography, *The Other Half,* Lord Clark
has some interesting comments on this friendship, record-
ing an impression that was shared by many others:

> There are lots of good people in the world who are simple, or
> even stupid, David was that rare phenomenon, a very good
> man who was complex and highly intelligent. He had a sweet
> smile, but also a penetrating glance which saw through any
> form of pretence. I knew it was an undeserved privilege for
> me to be in his company, but he was so easy to talk to that I
> forgot my sinful state. We talked about history, poetry and
> nature . . . on our walks in the valleys behind the Castle, he

would pause before a tree or a turn in the valley and say 'This is good!' He meant more than 'I'm enjoying it'. Good meant to him that it was the work of God.

During these years friendship meant much to David. He had once written to me that he could never drift away from people who had been close to him. Ailred of Rievaulx had once written much the same: *Semel a me receptus in amicitiam a me nunquam poterit non amari*. A letter written to David after his retirement gives an impression of the influence his personality had on a much younger colleague in the Faculty of History:

> ... I, at least, cannot say to you in person quite what I want to, partly from awe, but from an intense respect for your 'reserve', which means that in one sense at least you remain an enclosed contemplative (or that is how I see it) and that is partly what makes you what you are and what I (and many others) admire so much. It is not grim or forbidding: it is just an 'otherness' which makes me sometimes want to fall on my knees and ask your blessing but at the same time prevents my doing so! ... But so often the barriers of conventionality, shyness and whatever, together with the fact that the world has debased the coinage result in our stopping short of telling our nearest and dearest of our love. I could not tell you, for all these reasons, how much I owe you.

My own relations with David had been re-established in the 1950s when we had been brought together at a lunch with Professor Edwards, then Director of the Institute of Historical Research. However, we rarely met or corresponded until my return to Cambridge in 1969. Hearing that I was to take charge of Benet House, David wrote to welcome my return, adding a comment on the Cambridge scene of that time:

> You will find the ethos—and particularly the R.C. ethos— very different from even ten years ago. My own experience, for what it is worth, is that taken as individuals (and abstract-

ing from clothes, hair, and girl and boy friends etc.) the
young are as pleasant as ever to deal with, but one has to
allow for a wide 'generation gap' on a whole series of important topics in which you don't talk the same language. This
came quite suddenly about four years ago, when the public-
and grammar-school code of behaviour and *Weltanschauung*
was swamped by boys and girls from the endless streets and
comprehensive schools of Chorlton-cum-Hardy, South
Shields, Peckham and other such resorts. They very often
know more than we do of modern literature, art and music,
and politics, but almost nothing of our deep roots of tradition. . . . I recall that it is 41 years almost to the day since I
learnt that I was to be sent to Benet House to replace Dom
Bede Camm. There are many 'what would have happened
ifs' in history.

When David visited Cambridge during my first term he
came to lunch at Benet House, the first time for thirty
years that he had entered it. Thereafter we met and corresponded regularly and I dined as his guest at Peterhouse.
The passage of the years seemed to have changed him
little: the quiet voice, the slight figure, the sympathetic
personality, all recalled the Father David with whom I
had tramped the Mendip Hills and had had eager discussions in a different age. His attitude to Downside seemed
to have mellowed and the old bitterness to have gone, and
he had restored good relations with other members of the
community, including Abbot Trafford. He also enjoyed
such opportunities as came his way to meet young monks
of the different abbeys and to encounter undergraduates:

Tomorrow I go to lecture to the history people at York. At
the moment one almost fears to meet a group of 'students'
and one is almost ashamed to talk about anything so non-
actual as medieval history. Will they riot and shy bags of
flour? Or will they just go to sleep like their predecessors?
Actually at Cambridge last week they seemed as mild as
mice—hirsute and shockingly dressed, but polite and nervous
as you could wish.

He enjoyed reminiscing about the past, occasionally touching on the one topic I would not myself have raised, his divergence from the rest of us in the community, and he wrote affectionately of friends. In 1974 he mentioned a visit he had received from Giles Constable who was about to spend a sabbatical year from Harvard as visiting Fellow at Churchill College:

Years ago I supervised him for a year on Peter the Venerable. Get to know him, if you do not do so already. He is a delightful person with a pleasant wife. I'm sure you would like him and vice versa. I was saddened by the tragic death of Helen Clover (another student of mine). Both as a scholar, a Catholic, and a person she was a personality, admirable in the way she worked for her sons (as a young widow), and for her scholarship afterwards. . . . It is 60 years in a few days since I was clothed in the habit as a novice at Downside. Quite apart from my arrival(!) it was a moment of destiny for Downside which we did not realise. I remember counting 45 monks in the *Statio* for vespers—the full blossoming of E.C.B.'s first term of office and the novitiate at Downside—so soon to feel the blast of World War I and all that has happened since. I often wonder what the presence of Stephen Hewett[1] would have made in the community after the war. He was the admirable Crichton—body, mind and soul—the most winning personality and simplest, sanest character and deepest lover of Downside. The school at Downside had its deep lovers (*et in Arcadia ego*) in those days.

There were changes in the life of the Church and in the monastic world after the second Vatican Council, to which David was unsympathetic. He wrote to a friend in 1967:

[1] Stephen Hewett: Downside 1905–11, Head Boy, Captain 1st XI, Balliol Scholar. Oxford 1911–14, Craven, Hertford, Ireland Scholar, Hockey Blue. Killed in action 1916. Author: *A Scholar's Letters from the Front*, ed. F. F. Urquhart. He had hoped to join the community after the war

It seems to me that the monastic order will rapidly fall apart into two main divisions—one of the Cistercians and some Benedictines who retain a vocation and an understanding for the traditional monastic life, which needs recurrent reform and accidental changes, but not an essential change—and the other of those who increase active employments and decrease silence and prayer and seclusion to become an active order with a monastic slant. Perhaps there will be a third division—that of the true missionary monasticism, preaching by charity and prayer *in partibus infidelium*—with which every sympathy must be felt. But at the moment it is an iron age, in which one looks in vain for a prophet or a master in Israel, and cant and humbug are very much in evidence. I can now, as a historian, understand how England lost the faith *tempore Henrici octavi*.

Some of the problems that face modern monastic communities were discussed in his *Christian Monasticism* published in 1969, a book which David named as 'my testimony to the monastic life ... which, as Our Lord also knows I have so far as human frailty allows, faithfully defended.' He wrote to me when it was in preparation:

I feel a certain sadness at the prevailing *malaise* in monastic circles, which seems to go deeper than the endemic wish for something better than you've got. I have recently finished (after five years reading and writing) a volume on the history of the medieval Church,[1] and am now doing a fairly large paperback on monastic history over the ages. I mention this because in both cases I have had to stop up some holes in my knowledge, and to stand back and look at the whole picture. As a result, I have been in many ways encouraged. We have been here before. In Renaissance Italy, and again in France and Germany in the Age of Reason, there was the same flight from God, and the same loss of nerve and of belief in monastic values, *mutatis mutandis*. And the wheel came round again. But what the answer will be in the short run I know not. The big school (which would presumably survive the threatened integration) sets a monastic community a terrible prob-

[1] *The Christian Centuries*, with D. Obolensky

lem. . . . But anyhow, as one now with a memory of 65 years
of life, I am sure that for a viable monastic life there must be a
fairly stiff (though not necessarily austere) observance, a
fairly stable life, and an equality of observance for all. A
monastic life which does not at least move towards evangelical perfection will never be viable. There may well be fewer
monks in the century to come—but the monastic life will
never die.

The extensive liturgical changes of these years he found
unattractive and was relieved to find that he was not com-
pelled to cease celebrating the Tridentine Mass in Latin.
He wrote to me at Easter in 1971:

Future generations of monks and boys will be the poorer from
the loss of the old Holy Week, and I think future generations
will wonder how the Church could make such a sudden mas-
sacre of one of the great art forms of the world—the Latin
Roman Liturgy of word and music. I appreciate the pastoral
needs of the vernacular, especially in countries of non-
European civilisation, but the move should have been planned, not stampeded, and (in these pluralistic days) the Latin
liturgy and music should have been kept in monastic orders
and perhaps in cathedrals. (and other churches by
choice)—or at least as a real alternative.

It was also a great accidental disaster that the original
liturgical movement was first of all in the 1950s allowed to get
into the hands of rabid liturgical purists, and then since 1963
exploited by those who used liturgical scholarship as a blind
for de-sacralising and de-catholicising the liturgy. But you
mustn't think I am a bitter conservative. I am quite prepared
to accept what comes to us—save for doctrinal or moral he-
resy, and I don't mull over this. It is just Easter and the
memory of a High Mass at Downside comes over one,

> 'The memory of what has been
> And nevermore shall be'

at least in the same form.

David's outlook on life, and in this he had always been

consistent, was expressed in a letter of 1972 to Abbot Trafford:

> ... I am an unrepentant elitist—in life, in art, in social life,
> it is the saint, the genius, the aristocrat who must be there to
> attract imitation and raise the level. The very thought of an
> egalitarian or a 'pluralist' (i.e. truthless) society is killing.
> You see, old age makes us foolish—though in fact, when I
> meet the young, I never find them difficult. It may be only
> that the small class of journalists and broadcasters do most of
> the damage. In any case, we have our faith, and that is
> sufficient.

After our last meeting at Cambridge in 1974, shortly
before he died, David wrote on returning home:

> I greatly enjoyed our talk on Wednesday. You are the only
> person with whom I can talk freely about Downside. I some-
> times think—*si parva licet conponere magnis*—that Downside has
> been to me something like the Anglican Church to
> Newman—greatly loved with a sense of eternal gratitude, left
> perforce and unwillingly and then recollected in tranquillity.
> When in the U [University] L [Library] this visit I got
> immersed in the *Downside Review* and certain facts came into
> my view. Here are a few. That about the years 1946–1958
> there was an intense literary activity of all kinds. The *Review*
> was very highbrow and notable. Fr Alban was Novice Master
> for 12 years and a quarter of the community (before Worth
> was hived off) had been through his hands.... I turned up
> the pages of Lytton-Milbanke's [present Earl of Lytton]
> reminiscences of Downside (a contemporary of mine in the
> school but three years younger). In the most eloquent page
> he says that all his relatives went to Eton and Eton was
> clearly the best school in England *but* Downside had it every
> way over Eton on account of the religious atmosphere that
> went through the whole life there, and that this was due to
> the monks and their daily service of liturgical prayer....
> Forgive these 'wild and whirling' thoughts and let us pray
> that we may all—somehow—come together in love of Our
> Lord.

Soon after receiving this letter I heard one evening from Peterhouse that David had died quite suddenly of a heart attack. It was fitting that among the friends who gathered at his grave were monks of four Benedictine abbeys.

It is sad that he had not returned to Downside to see for himself that the life of prayer, which he remembered so well, continued as it always had done since the foundation of the community nearly four centuries ago. The modern boy in the school, like his predecessors, may be disturbed in his slumbers by the early bell for Mattins and turn over with thankfulness that he can sleep on. He cannot fail to be aware that in the Abbey church the chant of the monks rises on his behalf and is a sign that the house 'is alwayes watching to God'; day by day the tolling of 'Big Bede' reminds him that the conventual Mass is being sung while he is in class or prep. However strong the traditions of a monastic community may be it cannot avoid change as the centuries of its life pass, change in its work and in the details of its daily life. To adapt a thomist phrase, once dear to David Knowles, not to go forward is to go back. The one constant, and the one test by which any community must expect to be judged, is its spirit of prayer.

In his personal life David always remained faithful to the renunciation of his past. He did not travel abroad, read novels, smoke, attend the theatre or the cinema. He had watched television only twice in his life and then for only ten minutes. Apart from the news he listened only once a year to a radio programme and that was the annual carol service from King's College Chapel. Yet it would be wrong to imagine that he gave an impression of austerity and rigidity; his sense of humour was delicate and very evident, as was his sympathy for the young. As he himself commented, there are many 'ifs' in history and it is idle, if attractive, to speculate on them. He once remarked to me that he would never have left Downside had he not been sent away, but he retained to the end his faith in his monastic profession. Two passages from his writings on monastic history have always seemed to me revealing and, in some degree, applicable to himself. The first occurs in his sketch of Langland, in the second volume of *The Religious Orders in England* (p. 111): 'Of a truth he had a kind of nostalgia for the cloister, or for a golden phantasm of the cloister.' The second passage comes from the chapter on Erasmus in the third volume (p. 148): 'He retained throughout his life, at least on the subconscious level of his mind, not only a sense that an injustice had been done to him, but also the need to prove to himself that he had lost no opportunity for spiritual progress by abandoning the life of his profession.' Be that as it may, as an active member of his community he had enriched and inspired the lives of many of his brethren; as an exclaustrated member he was a source of inspiration and admiration to many others, often not of his faith. Few who came into contact with him failed to recognise, as he had once written of Abbot Cuthbert Butler, that here was a man *rectus ac timens Deum,* with the power to lift up the minds of others to God.

Chapter Eight

MONASTIC HISTORIAN

I have made no important discoveries and changed no
patterns.

D. K to J. H. C. A., 1964

During David's tenure of the Regius Chair at Cambridge
and during his retirement it was common to find reviewers
naming him as the most distinguished English medieval-
ist. He took a humbler view of his achievement, writing in
1964: 'I don't think that I have any illusions as to the work
I may have done. I cannot hold a candle to a Stenton or a
Douglas or a Powicke or a Mcfarlane—*nedum* to a
Maitland—as a "professional" historian; I have made no
important discoveries and changed no patterns.' To some
extent his achievement as a historian is a commentary on
his early life as a monk, and it may be useful to consider
some of the influences that led to the writing of *The Monastic Order*.

It has been noted that as a young monk David read
extremely widely in classical, English and foreign literature, and history. It would appear that it was the reading
of Macaulay that first turned his thoughts to the writing of
history and he came to him by accident, reading first the
Essays and then part of the *History* but regarding this and
others of the classical historical works, including Gibbon,
as a literary discipline. His first publication, in 1926, had

the American Civil War as its subject and in the preface he wrote: 'I can scarcely remember a time when the American Civil War did not charm me with a fascination for which I can give no adequate reason even to myself.' In that choice of subject we detect the influence of his father and the books that he found on his father's bookshelves. We can discount the impression made by a conversation with the ageing scholar, Edmund Bishop, when he was still a junior monk. *(The Historian and Character* p. xviii.) A single conversation, however well remembered, will not have a deep influence on a young man of nineteen years unless his tastes are already formed. Edmund Bishop's influence came at second hand, from the scholarly tradition which he had done so much to encourage among an older generation in the Downside community, and from the specialist library which he had bequeathed to the Abbey. Two members of the community had a lasting influence on him in this respect. The first, who had taught him some history in the school, was Dom Lucius Graham, an outstanding teacher in his prime, if not a scholar; the second was the learned Abbot Cuthbert Butler, an authority on monastic history of the early centuries. Some chapters of his *Benedictine Monachism* were delivered as conferences to the community and he always stressed the importance for a monk to have some field of serious study. It was at his suggestion that Dom Thomas Symons began a study of the tenth-century reform movement of St Dunstan which led to an edition of the *Regularis Concordia*. The young David Knowles was guided to a reading of Sackur's *Die Cluniacenser*. He was also of course aware of the interest taken in the medieval past by early seventeenth-century members of the restored English Benedictine Congregation, of the research into monastic records made by Augustine Baker with the help of Sir Robert Cotton, and of the *Apostolatus Benedictinorum in Anglia* published at Douai in 1626 under the name of Dom Clement Reyner. One other influence deserves mention, that of Dean Armitage Robinson of Wells, who took a friendly interest in the intellectual pursuits of the community.

After the end of the First World War Cardinal Gasquet came from Rome every year to spend part of the summer at Downside, but it is unlikely that the young David Knowles had any contact with him or at this time read his books. They were already suspect. It is now some ninety years since Gasquet, at the time a man already forty years old and without training, began to research at the British Museum and Public Record Office. In 1956 David took him as the subject of his Creighton Lecture at London University, by which time he was largely forgotten as a historian. The lecture is a polished and amusing piece of work. While doing full justice to Gasquet's failings, and to his capacity for carelessness which amounted in old age 'almost to genius', the lecturer concluded: 'if it is perilous to accept Gasquet uncritically, it is foolish to neglect or despise him.' He reminded his audience that Gasquet was the first to explore many of the records methodically, that he had a flair for discovery, finding important documents which other scholars had missed, and his work gave an impulse for much that was done after him. The lecture illustrates its author's gift of extracting interest, amusement and sober conclusions from what must have seemed at the time an unpromising subject.

It was David's unexpected good fortune to be freed from work in the school at Downside in 1928 so that he was well placed to begin serious historical studies. At first he thought of working on the Reformation period and read through the Stonor, Cely and Plumpton letters, but by July 1929 the decision had been taken to begin work on medieval monastic history. He began with Domesday Book and a solid reading of Maitland and Vinogradoff, and in August wrote to me from his home:

So far I have been very quiet at home—about three hours work every day on Domesday and Vinogradoff—but tomorrow I go to the southern cathedrals with my father and later hope to cross the narrow seas. I have this morning finished sifting the Domesday figures and am now in a position to tell you in five seconds the value of the property held by any religious house home or foreign in England—where held and the name of every manor—whether held *in capite* or sub. You could make yourself very useful by checking my figures—say on two important houses—say St Augustine's and Trin. (Chr. Ch.) Canterbury. I choose them because St A. has only one holding (in Kent) and Chr. Ch. only four (Kent, Sussex, Essex and Suffolk) but they are among the richest half dozen houses in England. . . . It would be of great help because my figures differ considerably from Corbett's.

By October he was reading the *Five Centuries of Religion* which Dr Coulton was then publishing. I had another letter in that month:

I'm still reading Coulton and he has made me very interested. I'm sure there is room for a general history of English monasticism 1066–1539. He (and other books and chronicles) make me feel more and more that life at a big Black Monk abbey from 1200 on must have been even more hard than life here—hard to reconcile, I mean. Still, weren't a good many of the vocations real? I have for some months bound myself (under all but a vow) not to write or study anything except English religious history. This time I mean it. Can't we ultimately combine? Two periods? My old dream was the Reformation in England 1500–1640. I now wonder whether that brings one too much across deep subjects (e.g. the Anglican formularies) which we know no more about than Coulton does of Catholic spirituality. On the other hand I must have something more exhilarating than the *Regularis Concordia*. Anyhow for the present it is enough to read. But think you also what may best be done with the resources at hand. . . . You must never be utterly swallowed in the school.

A postscript was added to this letter:

Isn't Coulton's mistake expecting too much? His only real admiration is for the Bernards—the very few who come at the right moment in the right place. But actually I am sure it is easier for the immediate followers of a saint to approach near to his achievement—but it's useless to measure by merely the outside result, the work done. Surely one must look deeper at the will and attitude to God within.

In his own life, as perhaps in his historical judgements, David was to move away from the stand taken in this letter. Like Coulton, he, too, came to expect too much from monasticism, both in its history and as a life to be lived by ordinary men.

At the end of the war he met Coulton at Cambridge for the first time and always found him courteous in personal relationships. As an undergraduate I also experienced Coulton's unvarying kindness and shared the cocoa in his rooms at St John's which David was offered in turn when he was invited to a spartan supper of the kind described by Sarah Coulton in her memoir. Coulton commented on *The Monastic Order* that it was as good a piece of work as one could expect 'from an O.S.B.'. When Knowles commented on Coulton he was understandably restrained but he gives evidence for dissenting from judgements offered in *Five Centuries of Religion*, and an interesting comparison is afforded by their treatment of the case of Abbot Wallingford of St Alban's. (G. G. Coulton, *Five Centuries of Religion*, IV, pp. 508–59; D. Knowles, 'The Case of St Alban's in 1490', *Journal of Ecclesiastical History*, III, pp. 144–58[1].)

The suggestion of a collaboration made in David's letter of 1929 was attractive but I was about to begin four years of theological study, and sustained historical work would be impossible. David embarked alone on his project and had the good fortune to have chosen a subject for which there was a mass of printed source material, most of it in the monastic library, including the Rolls Series. Travel for

[1] In his paper on 'The Last Abbot of Wigmore' David Knowles treated a subject which had also been discussed by Froude and Gasquet. *Medieval Studies Presented to Rose Graham*, ed. V. Ruffer and A. J. Taylor

the purpose of historical research on manuscript sources was something which conflicted with his views on monastic life as they were now developing. He referred to this in a letter of 1964:

> When I began, microfilms were unknown and photostats were only possible (at considerable expense) in very limited numbers. So I ruled out any subject that would imply travel, and I never visited even the British Museum until I lived in London. Actually that was one—though not the chief— reason for my choice of subject. It was quite clear that up to 1215 at least the printed sources were sufficient for a history of English monasticism. When I lived in London (and later at Cambridge) I took considerable soundings in unpublished manuscripts and came to the conclusion that while manuscript research was desirable and necessary for the history of individual monasteries and for full economic treatment, for a general history the value of manuscript research would bear no proportion to the time spent. It was either—or; and I judged that what activities I had could be used more profitably as they have been.

In the early days David probably underestimated the importance of a knowledge of palaeography and diplomatic as part of the historian's training. Writing to a student in the 1930s he advised him not to get 'side tracked' into a study of palaeography.

During his editorship of the *Downside Review* (1929–33) the results of his early work on the Rolls Series were published in the form of eight essays, covering the period 1066–1215 and treating such topics as abbatial elections, the growth of exemption, cathedral monasteries, and the diet of the Black Monks. They drew attention to aspects which had not previously received such treatment and began to be noticed by professional medievalists. The subject of exemption from episcopal control, for example, had not previously been investigated on this scale. In an address on *Academic History*, printed in 1962, he recalled the emerging picture as it appeared to him:

The documents showed two completely different situations, separated sometimes by more than a century: the earlier groups of charters were grants by Anglo-Saxon kings or the Conqueror of fiscal and other immunities, together with a prohibition addressed to all bishops forbidding their interference with the monks; the later group were papal bulls of the twelfth century, giving, with increasing definition and amplitude, exemption from episcopal jurisdiction and immediate subjection to the Apostolic See. Suddenly I saw a whole climate of ideas changing before my eyes; the purely secular, quasi-feudal protection of the king, standing wholly outside any Roman or canonical tradition, was suddenly replaced by the hand of the centralising Gregorian papacy and the machinery of canon law. The monks of Chertsey or Battle cared nothing for this; they were concerned solely in making sure of what the kings had given them. The popes, without a thought of the past, were concerned solely in defining the categories of their client churches. Yet one world had slipped into another; the *Eigenkloster* had become an abbey subject to the Apostolic See *nullo mediante*. . . . One great province of an historian's task is to isolate and comprehend such changes, economic, administrative, intellectual, in which, as in substantial changes of Aristotelian metaphysics, a form has changed upon a base that remains the same.

While preparing these essays for the *Downside Review* David was collecting material for *The Monastic Order* and it is on this work, and the three subsequent volumes of *The Religious Orders in England* that his reputation as a historian will mainly rest. The preparation had been completed by the time he moved to Ealing Priory in 1933 and by late autumn of 1937 the book had been written and typed. It was, therefore, a work of the cloister, owing little to libraries other than that of Downside. When completed it was a lengthy work of 800 pages, and when it was accepted by the Cambridge University Press, on the recommendation of Professor Hamilton Thompson, a condition was made that its length should be curtailed. About a hundred pages were therefore omitted, and these included chapters on monastic architecture, monastic

writers, and an account of Gilbert of Sempringham. The
chapter on monastic architecture was later printed in *The
Historian and Character*. David was fortunate in the publication date of *The Monastic Order* for few serious and scholarly
works were being published in 1940 and important
reviews appeared within a few weeks. It was an immediate
success and by 1941 the edition had sold out. Unfortunately the Press had not anticipated large sales and the
type was broken up after a printing of only 500 copies. A
photographic reprint was also soon sold out and the book
remained out of print for some years.

It is given to few historians to achieve such success with
a first medieval work of some 700 pages. The quality of
The Monastic Order was sensed at once by perceptive
reviewers such as Professor Powicke, most generous of
medievalists in his encouragement of beginners, and
Eileen Power. Several reviewers emphasised the depth of
understanding which resulted from the author's knowledge of monasticism from within, and many drew attention to the distinction of style displayed on every page.
Even the casual reader will appreciate also the wide range
of quotation and illustration, and the author's ability to
bring to life a historical figure or event that had suffered
from the dead hand of earlier writers. The immediate impression made by this book was summed up by Professor
Powicke: 'As a piece of impartial criticism and clear, sustained narrative, it reveals a new historian in the best
sense of the word.' In some respects it was the best of all
David's historical writing.

The Monastic Order was the work of a historian who knew
monasticism from within. It was also in preparation during a period when its author was himself undergoing a
crisis of conscience, and completed after he had seen the
disappointment of his plans for his own monastic future.
Abbot Cuthbert Butler in his *Benedictine Monachism* suggested that monastic history written by the reformer needs
to be regarded with reserve. When we weigh up the
generalisations of David Knowles it is as well, perhaps, to

remember that he looked on monasticism, past and present, from one definite point of view. Inevitably also there are passages which throw light on the author and we find one in the first chapter of *The Monastic Order*. He is commenting on the deep influence of the Rule of St Benedict:

> No other writings, save the psalms and the gospels, had a position in any way comparable to it. Even at the present day, when the volume of theological and spiritual literature is so enormous, and when every individual makes something of a selection for himself from the riches to hand, all those who have heard the Rule read each day over a period of years know that fragments and phrases lie in their memories and pass before their minds at moments of deliberation or crisis.

He mentions the judgement of Dom André Wilmart that John of Fécamp was the greatest spiritual writer before St Bernard: 'Those familiar with his prayers will scarcely question this judgement' (p. 86). Here David is not implying familiarity with the prayers as a historian. They were printed in the Roman missal of Pius V and attributed to St Ambrose; David would have read them through before celebrating Mass.

An account of the expansion of building activity that followed the Norman plantation includes a modern comparison: 'Only those who have lived in a great and growing establishment can fully realise the effect upon the mind of expansion into spacious buildings from small' (*The Monastic Order*, p. 121). We are told that Abbot de la Mare of St Alban's ruled by love and was never happier than when among his monks, staying often with those on holiday at the Redburn grange and sometimes ringing the bell for choir Office when those responsible failed to do so. A characteristic footnote adds that Abbot Cuthbert Butler of Downside (1859–1934) sometimes supplied a similar defect, and was known to have left a note on one occasion in an erring Junior's cell: 'Shall be away today. Please get another to ring the Angelus. ECB.' David has a passing reference to modern practice with regard to abbatial elec-

tions, and when he writes of the office of Cellarer he quotes
the constitutions of the English Benedictine Congregation
(*M.O.*, pp. 249, 309). Two passages are especially elo-
quent of past experience, the first of these on the Abbey
church at Gloucester:

> It would indeed be difficult to find a more admirable setting
> for a pontifical Mass than that spacious pavement bathed in
> light that would have fallen on cloth of gold, the lawns and
> linens and damasks, the silver candelabra and the rising
> clouds of incense. And perhaps only those who have known
> by long experience, year in and year out, what rest is given by
> natural light to eyes tired by glare and shadow will feel the
> full refreshment of Gloucester choir, and only those who have
> watched the dawn stealing upon the end of a long Office – *lux
> intrat, albescit polus, Christus venit*[1]—will know how the shafts of
> June sunlight over Cleeve brought hope and faith to many
> who saw that great window gleam in the level rays (*R.O.*,II,
> p. 37).

It is clearly evident again in the evocative passage
which was once intended as an ending for the third volume of *The Religious Houses in England:*

> How many generations of monks or canons ... in the cool
> morning of life, when the beauty of the external world strikes
> so suddenly and deeply into the mind as a revelation and an
> anguish, must have paused in the cloister to regard the si-
> lence and the glory of the December stars, or have met there
> the breeze of a spring morning, laden with the scent of may
> blossom or bean flower. ... In a building where a succession
> of men have passed from youth to age among the same towers
> and trees we seem for a moment to cross the abyss of time and
> to be upon the point of seeing with their eyes these lichened
> walls, once harbouring such a busy world of life and rever-
> berating to the sound of footsteps and the music of bells
> (*H.A.C.*, p. 211).

[1] Quotation from the hymn for Wednesday Lauds in the Monastic
Breviary

A monastic reader of these volumes will notice the occasional side blows at modern practice. Chaucer's monk exhibits 'the qualities found in monks by medieval satirists all over Europe and in every age, in various combinations', faults it is added that are all but endemic in the monastic body, and even in our own day 'there are those whose withers might well be wrung by Chaucer's lines.' With the third volume of *The Religious Orders in England* we come to the time when Jerusalem was searched with lighted candles and visitation made on men who were settled upon their lees—dissolution was at hand. Coulton had concluded that at this time the number of monastic servants was excessive but David Knowles judged that the sixteenth-century monk received no personal service or attendance so long as he remained in the monastery. He found no evidence of the services received in some modern religious houses such as the sweeping of cloisters, the making of beds, or cleaning of footwear. A comment on this was added: a modern monastic house 'may well set itself the ideal of dispensing with the ministrations of any paid servants' (*R.O.*, III, p. 264). Robert Aske's praise of the northern abbeys at the time of the Pilgrimage of Grace is not permitted to pass without comment: 'There are many religious houses of mediocre life in the modern world to which a well disposed layman would pay a similar tribute of praise' (*R.O.*, III, p. 328). At the end of this third volume the question is asked: 'what message for himself and his brethren would a monk draw from this long review of monastic history, with its splendours and miseries' The answer is a simple one and only in fidelity to the Rule can a monk or monastery find security:

> When once a religious house or religious order ceases to direct its sons to the abandonment of all that is not God, and ceases to show them the rigours of the narrow way that leads to the imitation of Christ in His love, it sinks to the level of a purely human institution. . . . The true monk, in whatever century he is found, looks not to the changing ways around

him or to his own mean condition but to the everlasting God, and his trust is in the everlasting arms that hold him (*R.O.*, III, p. 468).

All readers can appreciate the distinction of style and the wealth of quotation. It sometimes appears in the casual footnote and so, after discussing the seemingly heroic quantities of monastic beverages, the reader is reminded of the prudent reserve of Dr Johnson when questioned as to the thirteen bottles of port alleged to have been drunk at a sitting by Dr Campbell (*M.O.*, 717). Of Wyclif, no favourite of the author, it is remarked with a reminiscence of Newman's *Apologia*, that 'rue, not snapdragon clung to the walls of Balliol' (*R.O.*, II, p. 106). Sophocles, Euripides, Virgil, St Thomas Aquinas and St John of the Cross are among authors drawn upon by way of illustration and comparison. Of Jocelin of Brakelond we are told that 'out of an ocean of froth' he had a singular talent for preserving opinions common to all types of character throughout the ages:

Jocelin has in this respect a certain kinship with the fifteenth idyll of Theocritus, with the conversations of Bottom and his friends, with the talk of the company in the parlour of the Rainbow, and with that of the worthies of Mellstock, save that in all these cases the writer is also a critic.

Two passages illustrate the distinction of style and have often been quoted. The first comes at the end of an account of Henry of Eastry, cathedral Prior of Canterbury:

To Eastry, the primroses of the Kentish brookland, the harebells and ragwort of the downs, the whispering reeds and dazzling levels of Thanet were familiar sights, but of such things he does not speak, and perhaps did not think. He saw the pastures with the eyes of Shallow, not with those of Perdita; his thoughts worked the round of market prices. . . . Stiff, dry, masterful, he passes before us as he rides about the manors or sits in the exchequer. He died, still active, while celebrating Mass in April 1331 (*R.O.*, I, p. 54).

The second passage, from a commentary on the *Rites of Durham*, comes near the romanticism against which the author has warned us:

> Whatever their life may have held of ease and mediocrity the beauty of the setting remained, and the display on high days and holy seasons of the treasures of artists and craftsmen that the centuries had accumulated. The lights still 'did burne continually both day and night' in the great cressets before the high altar, in token that 'the house was alwayes watching to God', and the sound of bells at midnight ... clear in the magical silence of midsummer or borne fitfully across the Wear in winter storms, gave assurance to the townspeople and the countryside 'in the deep night that all was well' ... The old conservative did not live to see the final desecration ... but he had seen the shrine and the pyx disappear. The glory had departed from Durham, for the ark of God had been taken away. (*R.O.*, III, p. 136–7).

A strong sense of the *lacrimae rerum* is evident throughout, notably in the volume on the Dissolution, but is accompanied by a robustness and austerity of judgement not all that far from the judgements of a Coulton, although the manner of presentation is indeed very different. I have mentioned the postscript to the letter of 1929: 'Isn't Coulton's real mistake expecting too much? His only real admiration is for the Bernards—the very few who come at the right moment and in the right place.' Ten years later one senses a similar approach in *The Monastic Order;* its author's preferences are very clear. In their early days of fervour and strict observance the Cistercians, and in all ages the Carthusians, are preferred to the Black Monks. Of St Bernard's sanctity he writes: 'It is the only significant thing about him,' and although he quotes the saying of Ailred of Rievaulx that the Cistercian way of life was not intended to be a garden enclosed in which only rare and pure souls would find green pasture, all monks of whatever kind are judged by their ability to reach the heights. So we are told in *The Monastic Order,* p. 224:

> the few religious institutes which have endured through centuries with their purity all but unimpaired—the Carthusians and the Carmelite nuns of the Teresian reform are examples—have done so, humanly speaking, because to a rigid observance and an unchanging Rule they have added a most rigid and exclusive selection and probation.

Medieval man was little given to self-examination or introspection in his writings and we can usually only guess at the quality of his attitude to 'God within'. These four volumes afford interesting examples of generalisations and particular judgements which seem to result from the application of a remarkably élitist standard of measurement. Dependent priories, we are told, however regular, lacked a fully responsible head and so 'could never fully realise the life of the Rule'. That might be true of particular instances, but as one who lived for a short time in an observant dependent priory I would regard it as a false generalisation. Again it is claimed that local customs lowered the standard of fervour by recognising a respectable regularity as the norm for all instead of throwing the road open to a higher achievement (*M.O.,* pp. 687, 688). The final page of *The Monastic Order* proclaims the ideal:

> Unless it gives to those who enter it an invitation to the highest perfection, together with the doctrine and discipline without which in the normal course that invitation cannot be followed, a religious institute must be pronounced a failure, and unless a monk, in his years of maturity, live in spirit apart from the world, with all his powers dedicated to the love of God, he must be pronounced unfaithful, in greater or less degree, to his profession (*M.O.,* p. 693).

Individuals as they pass across these pages are subjected to severe examination. Thus we are told of Thomas

de Marlberge of Evesham that despite being an exemplary
abbot, a man of piety and good intentions, he was a monk
of 'no spiritual depth'. Prior Eastry of Canterbury is
judged unlikely to have passed through the darkness and
light of spiritual progress and of the austere and observant Abbot Thomas de la Mare of St Alban's there is the
comment that 'we may perhaps be allowed to feel that the
ultimate touch of holiness is wanting' (*R.O.*, II, p. 48; I,
p. 54). Thomas of Brunton was a Norwich monk who
became Bishop of Worcester, a conscientious bishop who
was also a learned and fearless preacher. He is described
as a type of monk bishop that occurs throughout the ages
and is compared to two ninteenth-century monk bishops,
Ullathorne and Hedley. All three are judged to have had
'a solid piety that never blossoms fully into sanctity' (*R.O.*,
II, p. 59). Abbot Clown of Leicester is judged to have been
a man of respectable piety but not one of deep spirituality,
while Richard Whytford, one of the author's esteemed
Bridgettines, is deemed to have had 'a kind of spiritual
timidity and tenuity' (*R.O.*, III, p. 214). Whole-hearted
admiration is withheld until we come, at the Dissolution,
to the Carthusians.

After an account of the martyrdom of the first six the
story is told of the petty persecution endured by the rest of
the community of the London Charterhouse before the
end, when two servants of Cromwell were put in charge.
The monks were deprived of their books, and the curriculum disorganised by the daily exhortations of Council-
lors and other visitors. Ten more of the monks were
removed to Newgate and systematically starved to death.

> Rarely indeed in the annals of the Church have any confes-
> sors of the faith endured trials longer, more varied or more
> bitter than these unknown monks. They had left the world, as
> they hoped, for good; but the children of the world, to gain
> their private ends, had violated their solitude to demand of
> them an approval and a submission which they could not
> give. They had long made of their austere and exacting Rule

a means to the loving and joyful service of God; pain and
desolation, therefore, when they came, held no terrors for
them. When bishops and theologians paltered or denied, they
were not ashamed to confess the Son of Man. They died
faithful witnesses to the Catholic teaching that Christ had
built His Church upon a rock (*R.O.,* III, p. 236).

Surprisingly on the final page of this volume we are
reminded of the warning of the liturgy that, in judging, the
reader must be mindful of his own proper state and condition.

Two Oxford historians noted this severe search for perfection from necessarily imperfect men. William Pantin of
Oriel described it as a process resembling that of an
examination board in session. Beryl Smalley, in a review
of the *English Mystical Tradition,* compared its verdicts with
those of the earlier *English Mystics.*

> Rolle stands where he did before; he gets a distinction in
> prelims which he mistook for schools. The author of *The Cloud
> of Unknowing* might still get a first if he could be viva-ed.
> Hilton and Dame Julian are high seconds, Margery Kempe,
> the new examinee, fails university entrance. Baker drops
> below his former place; he now has a teacher's certificate.

In his Inaugural Lecture as Regius Professor, delivered
in 1954, David Knowles claimed that the historian must
be able to judge between uprightness and sanctity but it is
questionable whether the historian is equipped and competent for this difficult task. In this rare atmosphere some
may feel inclined to use the professor's own quotation
against him and feel that we cannot

> take upon's the mystery of things
> As if we were God's spies.

Seven years after this lecture *The English Mystical Tradition*
contains a relevant sentence on the seventeenth-century

Augustine Baker: 'Three centuries after a life has been lived, no one would wish to pose as a competent judge of the finer shades of its significance.'

The four monastic volumes have been treated in some detail for they not only represent the author's *magnum opus* but also reveal something of his personality, more so perhaps than any of his other writings. *The Monastic Order* is also a splendid example of narrative history and brings the past alive with a masterly touch which surpasses the second chapter of Powicke's *Stephen Langton* or the pages of G. M. Trevelyan on St John's College at Oxford during the Civil War. To many *The Monastic Order* will seem the finest of the four books, but the final volume of *The Religious Orders in England,* a far more difficult subject, comes not far behind. They are naturally not wholly free of defects, both of plan and omission. Galbraith noticed in the final volume its 'naïve, uncomplicated hypothesis of an age of perfection, far in the past, which with the coming of a fuller historical record, gradually fades into the light of common day.' It has also been remarked that while we are given full and detailed accounts of, for example, Prior More of Worcester and Prior Eastry of Canterbury we are told very little of the life of their communities and the daily round of the ordinary monk. It is, however, unlikely that the story will be re-written on this scale or with this distinction, although it will continue to be revised and supplemented. David Knowles inspired and stimulated many workers in this field, both colleagues and pupils, and much remains to be studied, especially on the economic side. The monograph of R. B. Dobson on the cathedral Priory of Durham during the fifteenth century shows how much remains to be learnt from unprinted records.

If David Knowles tended to be over-positive in some of his generalisations the Birkbeck Lectures of 1962 are typical of his willingness to admit error or the need for revision of earlier work. They also illustrate his ability to take up a complicated subject outside his own specialist field and disentangle the argument in clear and simple language.

The problem was the relationship between the Rule of St Benedict and the Rule of the so-called Master. This was a controversial subject that had attracted contributions in six languages, covering some thirty periodicals, and was largely unknown in this country until the end of the war opened up scholarly relations with the continent. In the first chapter of *The Monastic Order* the common view of scholars was adopted which regarded St Benedict as a legislator 'of great originality and creative genius'. A study of the discussion which had exercised scholarly circles abroad after 1937 led, however, to a different conclusion. It was accepted in the Birkbeck Lectures that St Benedict's originality cannot be upheld today, and that he made extensive use of the earlier Rule of the Master. [1]

The historical work of David Knowles was, of set purpose, concerned with the Christian tradition of the past and its link with the ancient wisdom of the classical inheritance. As a monk and a priest he felt it his duty to concern himself, not with apologetics, but with history in which Christianity was taken for granted as true. He also believed that for the man who would penetrate and understand the truths of faith and the ways of God, a knowledge of history is, after the study of the scriptures and theology, the most valuable of all mental possessions.

[1] Considerable attention has been given to this question since 1962. See B. Jaspert, 'Die Regula Benedicti—Regula Magistri—Kontroverse', Supplementa zu den *Regulae Benedicti Studia*, vol. 3, 1975

Appendix I

WRITINGS ON MYSTICISM AND PRAYER

Throughout a life of devoted historical work David Knowles maintained an interest in theology and contemplative prayer. He was not a trained theologian and had followed no university course of theological study. The exigencies of wartime had limited his theological studies at Downside and the final year in Rome had served to broaden his outlook and culture rather than to deepen his theological grasp. He had, however, an interest in speculative reasoning, had secured a sound basis from the philosophy of the classical Tripos at Cambridge, and in time he acquired a useful working knowledge of the *Summa* of St Thomas Aquinas. He was also able to fill gaps in his knowledge during the five years of teaching dogmatic theology at Downside, although as a teacher he kept closely to the textbook. In time he added an extensive knowledge of the works of St Teresa of Avila and of St John of the Cross, of the *Cloud of Unknowing*, and of Augustine Baker's *Holy Wisdom*. These he re-read every year, and it is characteristic of his thoroughness that he studied the work of the Carmelite mystics with the aid of the best Spanish text.

Two early letters reveal his current reading. The writings of Baron von Hügel are mentioned in a letter to me of 1930:

> I have been reading lately ... Baron von Hügel's *Letters to a Niece*. I wonder have you read it. To me it is the most impres-

135

sive book that I have read for six months or more. You have
there, it seems to me, the Baron at his best – neither too
metaphysical (as in parts of the *Mystical Element)* nor too
'dating', as in many of the letters to Tyrrell. You have the
mature, old, mellow Baron, handing on the torch—both
intellectual and spiritual. And what a vast sweep he
covers—Plato, Tertullian, Augustine, Bernard, Teresa, Milton, Shakespeare, Kant, Faber, Bradley, and the inevitable
Troeltsch—they jostle each other in successive letters, and
Greek numismatics comes next to Huvelin and the Prayer of
Quiet. It is an immensely stimulating book, and his judgements are almost unerringly sound—that is, they agree with
mine—and he has, with St Augustine and so few others, both
mind and heart. How typical that he should rest almost
under the shadow of Downside, and that the community
should not have been at his funeral—I wrote typical, but no,
it is not really typical of Downside. What is characteristic of
Downside is that it was to her he looked always as the most
sympathetic home of religion in England.

Three years later he wrote a similar letter to his cousin,
Dame Katharine Loxton:

> ... I read St John and St Thomas *de Verbo incarnato* for Lent,
> and mean to go on with St Thomas till I have read all the
> *Summa*. Since Easter I have been reading Maritain's latest—
> and greatest—book, *Les degrés du Savoir*. It is a masterpiece of
> thought and theology. His aim is to separate and safeguard
> every degree of the Mind's knowledge, according to the doc-
> trine of St Thomas ... and he ends up with a magnificent
> hundred pages on St John of the Cross.

The influence of Abbot Cuthbert Butler can be detected
in a first publication, *The English Mystics* of 1927. Three
important articles on contemplative prayer followed in
1932, the fruit of his reading of the Spanish mystics and of
experience gained from Retreats given to nuns. They were
published anonymously in the *Clergy Review*. In a letter of
this·year to one of his Junior monks he wrote:

I have just been reading the *Interior Castle*. It represents, as you know, St Teresa's latest word on the stages of the spiritual life, but she deals with the lower degrees very summarily and I think for all those who are not *in excelsis* it is the least helpful of her books. But it ought to be read—and re-read. The *Life* is much more practical. I read the *Interior Castle* this time with an inquisitive eye to see if (as the Jesuits and the Abbot say) you can really drive a wedge between her and St John. Actually I could find nothing which was incompatible with St John's (the correct) viewpoint, though several bits were put in a way he would never have put them.

In 1934 he published two articles, one on 'Contemplation in St Thomas Aquinas' and a second on 'The Excellence of the *Cloud*', a work whose author he judged had claims to be considered 'the most subtle and incisive, as well as the most original, spiritual writer in the English language'. From this year until 1958 there is a gap, possibly due to the claims of his historical work but probably due to his equivocal ecclesiastical status. The silence was broken by an article on Father Baker for the *Clergy Review* of 1958 and by the publication of two books, *The English Mystical Tradition* (1962), and *What is Mysticism?* (1967). The first of the two books is an attractive and mature re-writing of the early *English Mystics* and contains some interesting re-assessments. The second is a somewhat arid work which might not find many readers today. A criticism of this book which seems to ignore the increasingly biblical theology of our time is to be found in Dom Illtyd Trethowan's *The Absolute and the Atonement* (1971) where the meaning given by Knowles to theological mysticism is accepted, but the philosophical views which underlie his theologising are found unsatisfactory. In the view of this critic the implication that there is no conscious union with God until faith has developed into a stage which alone can be termed 'mystical' makes the certainty of faith unintelligible. It may discourage those who genuinely seek God. It is not surprising that David Knowles changed or modified in later writings some earlier judgements. This is noticeable in his writings on Father Baker and some of his later judgements have been criticised in Antony Low's *Augustine Baker* (New York, 1970). There was also a change of emphasis in his opinion of de Caussade. In a foreword to Algar Thorold's edition of *Abandonment to Divine Providence* (1933) Knowles numbered de Caussade among the 'surest and most inspiring of spiritual teachers'. In a letter of 1967, criticising the 'innocent semi-quietism' of an article on contemplation in Nelson's *Catholic Dictionary,* he wrote:

> I am sure Père de Caussade, though himself fundamentally orthodox and traditional, has been an instrument of harm to many souls. I would never recommend his writings, save perhaps *L'Abandon,* to anyone of whose absolute sanity of spiritual judgement I was not sure. The teaching of St John and St Teresa is clear and true, that the true prayer of simplicity is one of loving attention to God as known by faith.

The study of Abbot Cuthbert Butler, reprinted in *The Historian and Character,* criticised the Abbot's *Western Mysticism* for a lack of theological and spiritual precision. This was an echo of criticism made by reviewers at the time of its publication in 1922, but the criticism was more fully developed in a foreword to the re-issue of the book of 1965, and further criticism occurs in a paper on 'The Influence of Pseudo-Dionysius on Western Mysticism' printed in *Christian Spirituality: Essays in Honour of Gorden Rupp* (1975). Some of the criticisms were refuted by one authority, E. I. Watkin, who made an interesting comment, claiming that David Knowles revealed 'an unmistakeable attitude, not indeed of personal, but of doctrinal superiority'.

In the years that followed the second Vatican Council David's theological standpoint became dated, or unfashionable. There is no evidence that he followed the developing theology of our time or freed himself from a rigid thomism. His articles on *Humanae Vitae,* reprinted as a pamphlet for the Catholic Truth Society, reflected a conservative position that tends to be out of favour today. It is somewhat ironical that this last effort in the field of moral theology won him a letter of commendation from an eminent member of the Roman Curia.

Appendix 2

ON MONASTIC OBEDIENCE

The Sarum Lectures of 1964–5, printed with the title *From Pachomius to Ignatius,* end with a sketch of the evolution of the teaching on religious obedience throughout the period. In view of David Knowle's own history it is of some interest.

He sets out first the 'accepted doctrine of ascetic theology'. The aim of the Christian is to do the will of God; in order to do it we must know it, and one means of this comes from those commissioned by the Church to teach. An ultimate sanction for religious obedience lies in the need for human help, by instruction and command. Obedience is an ascetical benefit but also a practical necessity. Part of our obedience must be given to men who represent God in our lives yet 'no man *qua* man, is wholly wise or wholly good; he is not therefore to be obeyed or believed in all conceivable circumstances.' Hence the problems that surround the teaching of masters of the spiritual life when they treat of obedience.

For the early Middle Ages the doctor of obedience is St Benedict, as seen in his Rule. The Rule is an 'abbot's Rule' but the monks are protected by several safeguards from the dangers of absolute government. St Benedict sees obedience in its simplest and most primitive form, he did not envisage the complicated situation resulting from the Rule's being slighted by both abbot and monks. 'The attitude towards obedience, rendered classic by the Rule ... had its obvious excellences ... it had, however, certain disadvantages.' By concentrating attention on the spiritual value of unreflecting obedience it encouraged a subjective attitude of mind which made obedience the one and only means of ascertaining God's will. 'The Rule takes no account of the psychological fact that to obey from subservience or indolence or lack of principle is a fault as common as disobedience.'

St Bernard was an apostle of monastic obedience but as a recruit from an exodus or break-away from an existing abbey he could not preach total obedience to Rule-abbot-custom. The individual monk now 'had a duty, under certain circumstances, of examining the abbot and the traditions of the house, and of departing if they were found wanting.' St Bernard's statement of the principle is quoted (p. 78): 'He who has taken vows cannot ... be kept from realising what he has vowed.' Therefore if a monk feels conscientious scruple let him depart from his own monastery to a house where the Rule is kept in its purity. The one who goes must not condemn those who stay, and the latter should not condemn the one who seeks a stricter life. David Knowles then asks the question: is this advice spiritually helpful? Is there not a level of observance beneath which observance of the evangelical counsels is not possible?

In a paper on Franciscan obedience and poverty he returned again to this subject, contrasting the approach of St Francis with that of St Benedict. Again he suggested that the latter concentrated attention on the spiritual value of unreflecting obedience 'before the value of ascertaining and accomplishing the declared will of God'. St Francis, he claimed, desired the brethren to obey the Superior in all good things, but if the Superior commanded something contrary to what the subject knew in his heart was right, he was to refuse obedience and abide by the consequences.

One may feel that this question of obedience in the religious life was one that David Knowles could not discuss except in the context of his personal dilemma. In a letter to one of his followers in September 1934 he wrote:

> So much has been said and written to me in the past months
> which uses great words, but wrongly. When the word obedi-
> ence is used we must not be afraid as of a kind of spell, but
> look at it as piercingly as we can. Very often beneath it lies a
> purely human conception. As you know well, there is no short
> cut, no short circuit, that avoids the ultimate claim and
> struggle between God and the soul.... Obedience (see the
> excellent articles in the *Summa*) is merely a means, and as
> soon as it leads away from, not towards its end, it becomes
> preposterous.... Do you remember the episode in the life of
> St Thérèse of Lisieux when she had to cling to the banisters to
> pull herself past the Prioress' room? The ordinary reader
> supposes that she was overcoming a sentimental affection for
> the Prioress. No. Look at the dominating, monopolising
> character of Mère M. de Gonzague. What Thérèse was over-
> coming was that desire—so natural in a humble soul—to
> throw itself at the feet of one clothed with authority and hand
> itself over entirely—apparently by an act of spiritual annihi-
> lation, actually by an act of very human cowardice.
> Remember her words when the same Mother made (from
> human motives) a demand for sacrifice from a novice, and
> the other nuns said—'Yes, a sacrifice, it is always good for a
> novice to make sacrifices.' And Thérèse, before all the com-
> munity: *'Il y a des sacrifices qu'on n'a pas le droit d'exiger.'*

Further comment appears in a letter of December 1935 to
Outram Evennett: 'In the last resort the mind can only
obey Truth ... St Benedict presupposes the cadres of the
monastic life, beyond which the abbot cannot move.
Beyond and above both is the true, spiritual obedience
which can only be given to one more enlightened than
oneself.'

Few religious communities could long exist on the basis
that true spiritual obedience can be given by the individual only to one more enlightened than himself, and few
commentators on the Rule would agree that St Benedict
concentrated attention on unreflecting obedience. The
Rule does not ask for blind or unreasonable obedience. St

Benedict's concept of obedience has been described as that
of the listening ear, the ready heart, to be interpreted in
the light of the Gospel. It does not exclude the personal
responsibility of the monk in forming and following his
own conscience. The approach of David Knowles to this
question in the Sarum lectures may be thought to be both
unbiblical and too literal. Consideration must be given to
St Benedict's modifications of earlier teaching on this subject, of the scriptural approach of the prologue to his Rule,
and his chapter on obedience needs to be studied in the
context of the Rule as a whole and not in isolation. Augustine Baker, himself no easy or conventional member of a
religious community held that the individual can never be
at liberty to plead private enlightenment against legiti-
mate external authority.

THE PROJECT FOR A CONTEMPLATIVE FOUNDATION: 1933

The End

As we are a group of individuals differing in age, character, and experience of the religious life, it is a little difficult to give without reserves any motives or desires which have affected all alike. But probably all would be ready to say that when they came to religion and throughout their religious life (whether long or short) they have felt called to a life of prayer, recollection and real hardship in God's service. Most would express this by saying that they have always felt called to a life fully monastic—that is, they would say, a life in which all the peculiar exercises, duties, aids and consolations of the monastic state are actually and permanently present, not only during the years of formation, but also throughout life; not only as a background, but also as the very breath of life. Some—those who are the oldest of the group in religion—would endeavour to express themselves with greater precision by saying that they have always felt dimly, and now feel clearly, that they have been called by God to the contemplative life, that is to say, a way of life whose chief occupation is the love and adoration of God in prayer, public and private. They would take the words of St Bernard: *Aliorum est Deo servire; vestrum adhaerere:* and would reply: *mihi adhaerere Deo bonum est.* They feel that such a life has always been encouraged by the Church, not least in our own day, and that there is room for such a life in the Church in England today. They would add that such a way of life ordinarily both requires and desires a real measure of separation from the world; it also demands and wishes for simplicity, roughness. Love without austerity would never be strong; and love will wish to follow Our Lord in poverty, however imperfectly.

The Reasons

We may perhaps be asked why it is not possible to realise this life, at least in great measure, at Downside? Setting aside all external and superficial reasons, the reply would be that the contemplative vocation is really different from the active, and that activities, distractions and satisfactions which are necessary and good for most are a hindrance to others—that is, are not what God wants of them. We should add that a whole series of circumstances has made it possible at Downside in the last twenty years, and particularly since the large novitiates began in 1923, for a novice with a contemplative vocation to be received here, and to enjoy during his years of formation almost all the helps and instructions necessary to develop that vocation. During the same period, on the other hand, Downside has considerably increased its activities. Hence [comes], when all accidentals are brushed aside, the origin of our group and its difficulties. We feel that in order to remain at Downside in the light of all that has happened, and of the facts as we see them now, we should either have to abandon all the motives and aspirations on which our whole spiritual life rests, or to endeavour to convert Downside to our point of view—and each of these alternatives is equally impossible and in fact morally wrong. The only course left therefore—since for a group of a dozen to go to some other monastery is not practicable, even if at all desirable—is to ask to make a foundation from Downside, and this, besides being the only alternative, seems to us when we look back over recent years, to be the end towards which God has been leading us.

The Proposed Scheme

Our proposal would therefore be to buy a house in a rural and preferably non-Catholic part of England, say East Anglia. The house should be large enough to hold at least twenty without additions, and it would be well if it had some possibilities of accommodating guests, retreatants etc., in small rooms. It should have attached to it, or at least very near, the buildings of a small dairy farm and piggery. It should have a large kitchen garden and well-stocked orchard, and land at least sufficient for pasture of a herd of cows. The aim would be to be as self-supporting as possible with dairy produce, eggs, vegetables and fruit, and perhaps in time to increase all these forms of produce for the market. Our wish would be to remain a fairly small community, producing for ourselves what we could by our own labour.

The Life of Prayer and Work

1 *The Divine Office*

Nihil operi Dei praeponatur. As this is the most important 'work' for Benedictines, the whole time-table should be arranged to secure the best possible choir observance. But while the Office as a whole should be recited fairly slowly (slower, that is, than at Downside), and as much sung as is reasonably possible, we should aim at keeping the ceremonies as simple as possible, so that the liturgy may be, as far as possible, pure prayer.

2 *Prayer*

With slightly more time spent in choir than at Downside, with very much more silence, and with work

entirely in the enclosure, it would probably be enough if
there were two fixed half-hours, i.e. morning and evening, in addition to the thanksgiving after Mass and a
daily (constitutional) visit to the Blessed Sacrament,
but there should be the possibility for everyone to
increase this by another half-hour taken out of reading
time on ordinary days, and on Sundays and feasts it
should be the regular practice for all.

3 *Lectio divina*

At least an hour should be allotted to spiritual reading.
There would be short remarks on matters of discipline
etc., after Prime, a weekly chapter of faults, and a
weekly conference.

4 *Work*

All work should be regarded as St Benedict regarded it,
merely as a means to the end, which is the perfection of
the soul of the worker. Work is of course absolutely
essential to the monastic life, not merely because the
monks, so far as possible, must earn their livelihood,
but because they must be kept occupied when not
directly engaged in prayer. But all work should be of a
kind compatible with a life of prayer, that is, allowing
the worker to remain really recollected as much as possible. It would, therefore, be carried on in the enclosure,
and be of a kind to allow the choir monks to leave it at
stated intervals for the conventual duties. Moreover,
there would be a variety of work, and this is where the
monastery we are contemplating would differ both from
other houses of the Congregation and also from the
Carthusians and Cistercians. We do not (as a group)
feel called to either of these latter lives, but we do feel
that we have a vocation to the contemplative life, and
this is the whole *raison d'être* of the foundation. No one,
therefore, who cannot live without the distractions of
activity should be accepted for such a house.

A foundation made from Downside would naturally endeavour to carry on, at least in a small way, the precious Gregorian tradition of scholarship and culture, and there are some in our group who could study, write and teach theology. They would have to be content, at least for many years, with far less satisfactory library facilities than at Downside, but here again they would put their vocations first. For others there would be the giving of Retreats to guests and groups of those who came, the instruction of converts etc. For others again there would be agricultural and garden work. It should be possible to run a small dairy farm, pig and poultry farm and garden. Finally, and this is most important, all those not physically unable would do their share of the house work and take part as a regular exercise in the garden or field work. In the first years, when some have still to complete their theology, there should be no difficulty whatever about employment, and later we can hope that experience would show in which direction lay the best hopes of development.

5 *Recreation*

An hour's recreation a day would probably be sufficient, since out-of-door work would be part of everyone's life. This hour would be after dinner, and a quarter of it would be spent by all the community together. The novitiate might add to this a short recreation after supper. There would be no smoking, wireless, gramophone, games etc. A single good newspaper and some of the religious and learned periodicals, but no merely literary or topical ones. Perhaps one or two afternoons a week it might be recognised that permission would occasionally be given for walks outside the enclosure for an hour or more. There would be no holidays, not even whole-day excursions, and no meals outside the enclosure even with relations. On Sundays and Feastdays there should be no more recreation (i.e. talking) but more free time for reading etc.

6 *Silence*

This is one of the essentials of the life. While the whole aim would be for a Benedictine rather than a Trappist silence, the rules and discipline have to be strict, though details and methods would have to depend on the goodwill and experience of the first years rather than on rules laid down ahead. There would be no talking at meals, even on Feastdays; all the interior of the house (except the calefactory and the cloisters at recreation time) would be a place of silence, and for conversation beyond the absolute necessaries of work permission would have to be obtained. But there would be no aiming at the semi-eremitical life; it is of the genius of Benedictinism that the members of a family know each other and learn from each other. And equally it is Benedictine that guests and visitors acquire a real personal knowledge of some at least of the monks.

7 *Food*

This should be simple but wholesome, and plenty of it, well cooked. Meat not more than once a day (with perhaps some additional abstinence days). At breakfast as much bread and butter and coffee as the individual requires; a full ordinary meal at midday; an optional drink of tea with dry bread in the afternoon; at supper a dish (fish, eggs, vegetables) followed by bread and cheese or jam or fruit. The regular fasts of the Church would be observed by all.

8 *Sleep*

There should be a clear seven hours of unbroken sleep possible for all—that is, a time-table making it possible for one who needed it to obtain twenty minutes or half-an-hour more. No 'long' sleeps, not even (ordinarily) for the priest singing the Mass. Obviously, infirmarian or Superior could give extra food or sleep when really necessary.

9 *Poverty*

The greatest safeguard of (Benedictine) poverty is to secure as much uniformity as possible. The life of such a house as we suggest does not necessitate much private possession. For books we would look entirely to the common library, where it would be possible to work; the furnishing of cells would be kept absolutely uniform and consist of the absolute minimum required. With regard to corporate poverty every care would be necessary to prevent the simplicity and unworldliness of the community life suffering. Consequently, even at the risk of running counter to the accepted (medieval and modern) Benedictine usage, we should not ever aim at acquiring a magnificent church, buildings etc. We would aim at simplicity in everything. Individual poverty would be as extreme as possible; community possessions not such as to give the impression of a 'comfortable' life.

10 *Enclosure*

This, like silence, is a very important point. The enclosure must be a real one, not merely a legal one. Clearly for men the entrance into enclosure can never be precisely the act, *semel pro semper*, that it is for women, but permission to leave the enclosure for a whole day or for a night would only be given in really exceptional circumstances, not, for example, to attend weddings, ordinations etc., of relatives or friends, or (normally) to preach, read lectures, or papers. An exception might be made to give *occasional* Retreats to enclosed religious. But, on the whole, to leave the world today is more than ever a *sine qua non* of the contemplative way of life. If such a life is accused of being selfish, we would reply that it would indeed be selfish if, having secured all material means of following our vocation, we did not endeavour to leave ourselves to attain the closest possible union with God; but, in so far as we earnestly strive after that union, we shall, besides our personal service of God, benefit others, not merely by prayer and good works, but by leaving all things to follow Christ, and so finding in our union of love with Him, something of His love for souls.

11 *Numbers*

Here again we should tend to depart from the common Benedictine practice. Most of us feel that the house should always be tolerably small—perhaps not more than twenty-five professed choir monks, and that growth beyond that, if it came, should result at once in a new foundation. All this, of course, is to count unhatched chickens, and in any case the number of vocations will probably always be small, but there is a feeling among us that it is well to assert at the start that we do not contemplate growing into a large community, because we feel:

a) that only in a comparatively small one is simplicity, uniformity, and the personal control of a Superior possible

b) that the particular 'external' work contemplated, viz. the evangelising of non-Catholic parts of England by contemplative monastic houses, is best achieved if those houses are small.

12 *Parish Work*

Our proposal would be, as we have said, to choose a non-Catholic part of England to aid the spread of the faith, but it would be our rigid policy to do no external parish work. Perhaps some arrangement could be made with the bishop such as e.g. Cistercians have, that their church satisfies for Sunday Mass, and some of the monks have diocesan faculties to hear the confessions of neighbouring Catholics. Communion to the sick and Last Sacraments are also taken to those near the monastery when necessary, but no further parochial work.

13 *Lay brothers*

These are an all-but essential part of the scheme. It is fairly clear that in a present-day Benedictine house the cooking, tailoring etc. cannot be done by choir monks. It is also essential that there should be one or two hands available for the farm at times when the monks would be in choir. Laybrothers would thus reduce expense; but more than this, they would preserve a completely religious atmosphere throughout the enclosure. There should not be any insuperable obstacle to gradually building up such a group.

14 *Recruiting*

This would be the ultimate test of success, but if God wishes the foundation to be made He will send novices. It would be essential that none should be taken without the signs of a contemplative vocation but this would appear fairly early in the novitiate, and the kind of life proposed would be a fairly severe test of it before solemn profession. We base ultimately all our trust and hopes on the fact that God has, as it seems, given an extraordinarily united vocation and spirit to our group. Clearly, it would be essential to have the novitiate in the house from the start—that is, once the original group had things working—and for this, permission from the Holy See would be necessary. This we think is the ONLY permission from outside necessary, and something similar was contemplated when Milton was being discussed, so it should not be impossible.

15 *Constitutional*

We cannot see that there is anything in the proposed scheme (which is only a first rough draft) *against* our constitutions, which nowhere say that a house MUST have either a school or parishes or both, and which lay down that all regulations as to work, food, amount of recreation etc. depend upon the individual Superior (cf. especially CONST 36, 55, 61, 77, 78); There would be no suggestion that the constitutional obligation of the vows to go outside the monastery if ordered should be cancelled. It would be understood that IF such a foundation were to be made, the Abbot of Downside would not straightaway send its members to parishes, and if in time it became independent the obligation could be either modified, or the President's dispensing power could be sought.

We realise fully that until such time as the House became independent all regulations, customs and official appointments would derive all their religious sanction from the Abbot of Downside.

BIBLIOGRAPHY

List of books written by Professor Knowles

A complete bibliography, including articles and reviews, will be found in *The Historian and Character* for the period 1919–62; and in the *Ampleforth Journal*, 1975, for 1962–74.

1926 *The American Civil War: A Brief Sketch*, Oxford, Clarendon Press

1927 *The English Mystics*, London, Burns, Oates

1929 *The Benedictines*, London, Sheed and Ward. Reprinted 1930, New York, Macmillan

1940 *The Monastic Order in England*, Cambridge University Press
The Religious Houses of Medieval England, London, Sheed and Ward

1948 *The Religious Orders in England*, vol. I, Cambridge University Press

1951 *The Episcopal Colleagues of Archbishop Thomas Becket* (The Ford Lectures 1949), Cambridge University Press
The Monastic Constitutions of Lanfranc, Latin text and translation, London, Thomas Nelson and Sons

1952 With J. K. St Joseph, *Monastic Sites from the Air*, Cambridge Air Surveys I, Cambridge University Press

1953 With R. Neville Hadcock, *Medieval Religious Houses: England and Wales*, London, Longmans, Green and Company

155

1954 With W. F. Grimes, *Charterhouse, The Medieval Foundation in the Light of Recent Discoveries*, London, Longmans, Green and Company

1955 *The Religious Orders in England*, vol. II: *The End of the Middle Ages*, Cambridge University Press

1959 *The Religious Orders in England*, vol. III: *The Tudor Age*, Cambridge University Press

1961 *The English Mystical Tradition*, London, Burns, Oates; and New York, Harper

1962 *Saints and Scholars*, Cambridge University Press
The Evolution of Medieval Thought, London, Longmans, Green and Company

1963 *The Monastic Order in England*, 2nd edition with new preface, Cambridge University Press
Great Historical Enterprises and Problems in Early Monastic History, London, Nelson
The Historian and Character and Other Essays, Cambridge University Press

1966 *From Pachomius to Ignatius: A Study in the Constitutional History of the Religious Orders*, Oxford, Clarendon Press

1967 *What is Mysticism?*, London, Burns, Oates

1969 With D. Obolensky, *The Christian Centuries*, vol. II: *The Middle Ages*, Darton, Longman and Todd
Christian Monasticism, London, Weidenfeld and Nicholson

1970 *Thomas Becket*, London, Black

1971 *Medieval Religious Houses: England and Wales*, revised edition, London, Longmans

1972 With C. N. L. Brooke and Vera London, *The Heads of Religious Houses, England and Wales, 940–1216*, Cambridge University Press

List of Articles

1919 'A Preface of Mabillon', *Downside Review*, XXXVIII, pp. 53–7

1924 'The Religion of the Pastons', *D.R.*, XLII, pp. 143–63
      'Italian Scenes and Scenery', *D.R.*, XLII, pp. 196–208
1926 'Sanderson of Oundle', *D.R.*, XLIV, pp. 59–69
1928 'Animus and Anima', *D.R.*, XLVI, pp. 55–66
      'The Thought and Art of Thomas Hardy', *Dublin Review*, CLXXXIII, pp. 208–18
1930 'The Mappa Mundi of Gervase of Canterbury', *D.R.*, XLVIII, pp. 237–47
      'A Greek August', *D.R.*, XLVIII, pp. 291–314
1931 'George Ambrose Burton, Bishop of Clifton (1852–1931)', *D.R.* XLIX, pp. 209–14
      'Essays in Monastic History 1066–1215. I. Abbatial Elections', *D.R.*, XLIX, pp. 252–78
      'Honest Iago', *D.R.*, XLIX, pp. 326–36
      'Essays in Monastic History 1066–1215. II. The Norman Plantation', *D.R.*, XLIX, pp. 441–56
1932 'Essays in Monastic History. III. The Norman Monasticism', *D.R.*, L, pp. 33–48
      'Essays in Monastic History, IV. The Growth of Exemption', *D.R.*, L, pp. 201–31, 396–436
      'Contemplative Prayer', The *Clergy Review*, pp. 177–88, 278–91, 366–82
1933 'St Wulfstan of Worcester (1008–1095)', *The English Way*, ed. Maisie Ward (London and New York, Sheed and Ward), pp. 65–80
      'Essays in Monastic History. V. The Cathedral Monasteries', *D.R.*, LI, pp. 73–96
      'Contemplative Prayer in St Theresa', *D.R.*, LI, pp. 201–30, 406–33, 611–33.
      'Essays in Monastic History, 1066–1215. VI. Parish Organisation', *D.R.*, LI, pp. 501–22
      'The Monastic Horarium, 970–1120', *D.R.*, LI, pp. 706–25
1934 'Contemplation in St Thomas Aquinas', (*C. R.*,) VIII, pp. 1–20, 85–103
      'The Excellence of the Cloud', *D.R.*, LII, pp. 71–92

'Essays in Monastic History. 1066–1215. VII. The Diet of Black Monks', *D.R.*, LII, pp. 275–90

'Abbot Cuthbert Butler, 1858–1934', *D.R., LII, pp. 347–472; 'Abbot Butler: A Memoir', pp. 347–440; 'The Works and Thought of Abbot Butler', pp. 441–65, and 'Abbot Butler: A Bibliography', pp. 466–72

'Bec and its Great Men', *D.R.*, LII, pp. 567–85

1935 'The Revolt of the Laybrothers of Sempringham', *English Historical Review*, L, pp. 465–87

1936 'The Case of St William of York', *Cambridge Historical Journal*, V, pp. 162–77, 212–214

1936 'Rashdall's Mediaeval Universities', *Dublin Review*, CIC, pp. 300–14

1938 'The Early Community at Christ Church, Canterbury', *Journal of Theological Studies*, XXXIX, pp. 126–31

'The Canterbury Election of 1205–6', *E.H.R.;* LIII, pp. 211–20

1940 'The Confessions of St Augustine', *The Tablet*, CLXXV (N. S. CXLIII) pp. 456–7

'Durham Books and English Scholars', *Dublin Review*, CCVII, pp. 94–112

1941 'The Humanism of the Twelfth Century', *Studies*, XXX, pp. 43–58

1942 'Some Aspects of the Career of Archbishop Pecham, I and II', *E.H.R.* LVII, pp. 1–18, 178–201

1943 'The Cultural Influence of English Medieval Monasticism', *C.H.J.*, VII, pp. 146–59

1944 'Some Developments in English Monastic Life', 1216–1336', *Trans. Royal Historical Society*, 4th Series, XXVI, pp. 37–52

1947 *The Prospects of Medieval Studies:* An Inaugural Lecture, Cambridge University Press

'Some Recent Advances in the History of Medieval Thought', *C.H.J.*, IX, pp. 22–50

1949 'Archbishop Thomas Becket: A Character Study' (the Raleigh Lecture); *Proceedings of British Academy*,

XXXV, pp. 177–205

1950 'The Last Abbot of Wigmore', *Medieval Studies Presented to Rose Graham*, ed. V. Ruffer and A. J. Taylor, Oxford University Press, pp. 138–45

1951 'The Censured Opinions of Uthred of Boldon', *Proceedings British Academy*, XXXVII, pp. 307–42

1952 'The Case of St Alban's Abbey in 1490', *Journal of Ecclesiastical History*, III, pp. 144–58
'Further Notes on Recent Advance in the History of Medieval Thought', *C.H.J.*, X, pp. 354–8

1953 'Saint Bernard of Clairvaux: 1090–1153', *Dublin Review*, CCXXVII, pp. 104–21

1954 'English Monastic Life in the Later Middle Ages', *History*, N.S. XXXIX, pp. 26–38
'Le régime de gouvernement', *La vie spirituelle*, Supplement, VII, pp. 180–94

1955 *The Historian and Character*, Inaugural Lecture, C.U.P., pp. 21
Cistercians and Cluniacs, Oxford University Press, pp. 32

1956 'Peter the Venerable', *Bulletin of John Rylands Library*, XXXIX, pp. 132–45
'The Reforming Decrees of Peter the Venerable', in *Petrus Venerabilis, 1156–1956*, ed. G. Constable and J. Kritzneck, Studia Anselmiana, Rome, pp. 1–20
'The Limits of the Law: Lex iniusta non est lex', *Blackfriars*, XXXVII, pp. 402–12
'Lex iniusta non est lex', *The Catholic Lawyer*, II, pp. 237–44

1957 *Cardinal Gasquet as an Historian*, the Creighton Lecture, Athlone Press, pp. 26
'Additions and Corrections to Medieval Religious Houses', *E.H.R.* LXXII, pp. 60–87

1958 *The Historical Context of the Philosophical Works of St Thomas Aquinas*, Blackfriars Publications, pp. 14
'Great Historical Enterprises. I. The Bollandists', *T.R.H.S.*, 5th Series, VIII, pp. 147–66
'English Spiritual Writers. I. Father Augustine

Baker', *C.R.*, XLIII, pp. 641–57

'The Need for Catholic Historical Scholarship', *Dublin Review*, CCXXXII, pp. 120–8

'The Matter of Wilton in 1528', *Bulletin of Institute of Hist. Research*, XXXI, pp. 92–6

'The Preservation of the Classics', in *The English Library before 1700*, ed. F. Wormald and C. E. Wright, Athlone Press, ch.VII, pp. 136–47

'Religious Life and Organization', in *Medieval England*, ed. A. L. Poole, Oxford University Press, vol. II, ch. XII pp. 382–438

'The Portrait of St Dominic', *Blackfriars*, XXXIX, pp. 147–55

1959 'A Characteristic of the Mental Climate of the Fourteenth Century' in *Mélanges offerts à Etienne Gilson*, Toronto, pp. 315–25

1959 'Great Historical Enterprises, II. The Maurists', *T.R.H.S.*, 5th Series, IX, pp. 169–87

'Some Enemies of Gerald of Wales', *Studia monastica*, I, pp. 137–41

'Nicholas Breakspeare in Norway', *The Month*, N.S. XXI, pp. 88–94

'Jean Mabillon', *J.E.H.*, X, pp. 153–73

'The Twelfth and Thirteenth Centuries', in *The English Church and the Continent*, London; Faith Press, ch. II, pp. 25–41

1960 *Lord Macaulay, 1800–1859,* Cambridge University Press, pp. 30

'Great Historical Enterprises, III. The Monumenta Germaniae Historica', *T.R.H.S.*, 5th Series, X, pp. 129–50

'St Benedict', *The Month*, N.S. XXIII, pp. 69–83

1961 'Great Historical Enterprises. IV. The Rolls Series', *T.R.H.S.*, 5th Series, XI, pp. 137–59

'The English Bishops, 1070–1532', in *Medieval Studies Presented to Aubrey Gwynn, S. J.*, ed. J. A. Watt, J. B. Morrall, F. X. Martin, Dublin, pp. 283–96

1962 'Academic History', *History*, XLVII, pp. 223–32

'The First Franciscan Century', *The Month*, N.S. XXVII, pp. 148–55

1964 'Notes on a Bible of Evesham Abbey', *E.H.R.*, LXXIX, pp. 775–7
Studies in Church History, ed. C. W. Dugmore and C. Duggan, ch. 3, 'Some Recent Work in Early Benedictine History', pp. 35–46

1966 'The Monks of Westminster', *The Listener*, 20 Jan., pp. 92–4

1968 'Peter Has Spoken: the Encyclical without Ambiguity', Catholic Truth Society, Do. 413
'Peter the Venerable: champion of Cluny', *J.E.H.*, XIX, pp. 213–17

1969 'Denifle and Ehrle', *History*, LIV, pp. 1–12
'The London Charterhouse', *Victoria County History: Middlesex I*, pp. 159–69
'Some Trends in Scholarship, 1868–1968, in the Field of Medieval History', *T.R.H.S.*, XIX, pp. 139–57
'Authority', Catholic Truth Society, Do 416
John Coulson, ed., *A Book of Saints*, ch. 3, 'Becket'
'Benedikt von Nursia: Vater des Abendlandes', *Grosse Gestalten Christlicher Spiritualität*, ed. J. Sudbrack and J. Walsh, Würzburg, pp. 74–87, 406

1970 'St Augustine', *The Diversity of History: Essays in honour of Sir Herbert Butterfield*, pp. 19–33, ed. D. Brogan
'Archbishop Thomas Becket—the Saint', *The Canterbury Chronicle*, 65, pp. 5–21
'Religious Poverty: the traditional approach', *The Way*, Suppl. 9, pp. 16–26

1971 'Grace: the Life of the Soul', *C.T.S.*, Do 436
'Authentic Charisms', *Ampleforth Journal*, LXXVI, pp. 54–61

1972 'Henry II's Supplement to the Constitutions of Clarendon', with Anne Duggan and C. N. L. Brooke, *E.H.R.*, LXXXVII, pp. 757–71

1973 'Crucifying the Flesh', *The Way*, 13, Jan., pp. 12–21
'This Century of Change', *The Tablet*, Nov.–Dec.

1973 'Christopher Dawson, 1889–1970', *P.B.A.,* pp. 439–52

1974 'William Abel Pantin, 1902–1973', *P.B.A.,* LX, pp. 3–14

'The Eltonian Revolution in early Tudor history', *The Historical Journal,* XVII, pp. 867–72

David Knowles also contributed to the *New Catholic Encyclopedia* articles on Becket, Benedictine Rule, Cuthbert Butler, History of Church (Medieval), Constitutions of Clarendon, England 597–1485, Gilbert Foliot; for the 15th edition, *Encyclopedia Britannica,* articles on Thomas Becket, St Benedict of Nursia, Henry II of England, T. B. Macaulay, History of Roman Catholicism (in part).

INDEX

Acton Burnell 6, 26
Agius, Dom Ambrose 29
Alcester 13
Ampleforth Abbey 29
Arnold of Rugby, Thomas 7
Arras, abbey of 2, 3
Australian foundation, project of 73

Baddesley Clinton 42
Bailey, Cyril 51
Baker, Augustine (1573–1641) 2, 3, 4, 34, 43, 54, 132, 135, 138, 143
Balliol College 40, 51, 87
Barlow, Dom Rudesind (1584–1656) 3
Beaudoin, Dom Lambert 44
Beccles 84
Belmont Abbey, Hereford 29, 35
Benet House, Cambridge 33, 38, 54, 109
Birdwood, Field Marshal Lord (Master of Peterhouse 1931–8) 100
Bishop, Edmund 8, 9, 36, 48, 118
Bless, Gervase de 20, 25, 26
Boase, T. S. R. 51, 63
Bowra, Maurice 105
Bradshaw, Augustine (1576–1618) 3
Brogan, Denis 102

Brooke, Professor C. N. L. 14, 102, 103, 104, 105, 108
Brooke, Rosalind 103
Brooke, Professor Z. N. 99, 102
Brookfield, Dom Paul 30
Browne, Hon. Dermot 20
Buckley, Sigebert (1517–1610) 1, 2
Burton, George Ambrose, Bishop of Clifton 50
Butler, Dom Cuthbert (Abbot of Downside 1906–22) 28, 29, 33–4, 38, 58, 81, 111, 118, 124, 136, 138
Butler, Dom Urban 29, 44
Butt, Bishop (of Cambysoplis) 42
Butterfield, Professor Sir Herbert (Master of Peterhouse 1955–68) 100, 105

Cam, Helen 39
Camm, Dom Bede 38, 39, 54, 64
Campbell, Harris (Fellow of Christ's College, Cambridge) 39
Caussade, Abbé de 138
Caverel, Philip de, Abbot of Arras 2
Chalmers, Lord (Master of Peterhouse 1929–34) 100
Chapman, Dom John (Abbot of Downside 1929–33) 39, 43, 61, 62, 66, 68, 70, 71, 74, 77, 78, 79, 81

163